Alex Blaszczysnki is Professorial Research Fellow in the School of Psychology, University of Sydney, and Director of its Gambling Treatment and Research Clinic. He is editor-in-chief of *International Gambling Studies*.

The aim of the **Overcoming** series is to enable people with a range of common problems and disorders to take control of their own recovery programme.

Each title, with its specially tailored programme, is devised by a practising clinician using the latest techniques of cognitive behavioural therapy – techniques that have been shown to be highly effective in changing the way patients think about themselves and their problems.

Many books in the Overcoming series are recommended by the UK Department of Health under the Books on Prescription scheme.

Other titles in the series include:

OVERCOMING GAMBLING ADDICTION

2nd Edition

*A self-help guide using
cognitive behavioural techniques*

OVERCOMING

ALEX BLASZCZYSNKI

ROBINSON

ROBINSON

First published as *Overcoming Compulsive Gambling* in Great Britain in 1998 by
Robinson, an imprint of Constable & Robinson Ltd

This edition published in 2017 by Robinson

Copyright © Alex Blaszczynski, 1998, 2010, 2017

1 3 5 7 9 10 8 6 4 2

The moral right of the author has been asserted.

A CIP catalogue record for this book
is available from the British Library.

Important Note
This book is not intended as a substitute for medical advice or treatment.
Any person with a condition requiring medical attention should consult a
qualified medical practitioner or suitable therapist.

ISBN: 978-1-47213-868-2

Typeset in Bembo by Initial Typesetting Services, Edinburgh
Printed and bound in Great Britain by CPI Group (UK) Ltd, Croydon CR0 4YY

Papers used by Robinson are from well-managed forests and
other responsible sources

MIX
Paper from
responsible sources
FSC® C104740

Robinson
An imprint of
Little, Brown Book Group
Carmelite House
50 Victoria Embankment
London EC4Y 0DZ

An Hachette UK Company
www.hachette.co.uk
www.littlebrown.co.uk

Contents

PART ONE:
About Problem Gambling

PART TWO:
A Self-help Cognitive Behavioural Approach
to Overcoming Problem Gambling

PART ONE

ABOUT PROBLEM GAMBLING

Prologue

'Sweating on the win'

My heart is pounding. I am standing on my toes, every muscle in my body tense as I watch the horses hurtling toward the finishing post. All I can think of is winning; winning just that amount of money that will let me draw even again. I just need this one piece of luck and I'll be free again. The last three races have cost me dearly, I'm down to my last few pounds and if I lose again, I know I'm in real trouble. Excitement, fear, panic – these are the emotions overwhelming me, all mixed in together, what a buzz. This is a real high. Look at them go, my horse is edging in front, I'm going to win, I know I am . . .

I had no intention of betting on the horses today. I'm sick of being behind all the time, borrowing money from friends for lunch, no money to take the kids out, the car needs repairs and Emma, my wife, wants to go on holiday this Easter. This has been going on for the last four years and at age twenty-seven, I should have at least some money to buy things for the family. Now was the time to be strong: I was determined without fail to pay this month's rent. Already two payments behind and some more bills to come, I kicked myself for betting last week when I already had the money. I should have known better. But then, when I read the form guide and saw that one horse I knew was a certainty running over its favourite distance and at those odds, I just had to grab the chance. A win of this size would solve all my problems. The thought of that win just wouldn't go away, running through my mind constantly. The urge to gamble was too great, nothing else mattered, I had to place that bet no matter what. No thought of the possibility that I could lose ever entered my head.

I felt bad about lying to my wife that I was called in to do some overtime. It was a bit risky, too, because she could ask for the money to buy Rachel the shoes she needed for school. But this was the only way to leave the house without suspicion. I'd kick myself if this horse won without me backing it. It happened before and I was really angry. I blamed Emma for making me go to that damn party. I would have been five hundred in front and not in this mess now. I'm not making the same mistake twice. Anyway, she'll be happy enough when I give her some of the winnings. What she doesn't know won't hurt her.

Gee, I hate that wave of numbness that comes on when you lose your last penny. That horse would have won if the damn jockey didn't pull it so early. His fault totally – but that doesn't make me feel any better. Look at what I've done: I'm behind again, I've lied to my wife, Rachel will miss out again. To make matters worse, what will I tell Emma about the supposed overtime pay? I know, I lent it to Peter, he *had to pay some medical bills for his wife. No question that Emma will swallow that one.*

This is getting out of hand. No more, I promise. I get nothing out of gambling except feeling miserable and down and I keep taking it out on the family. It's not fair, I should wake up to myself. No more, I promise for sure.

Yes!! The horse has won, I've done it! I knew I would, no sweat. Gee, I feel great, on cloud nine! Three hundred pounds, what a beauty, I'm on a roll here. I can pay the bills now. But listen, I could double this three hundred on the next race. With six hundred the next few rent payments would be easy. I will win again, I'm positive. Yes, I'll go for it. If I start losing, I'll stop when I'm down to two hundred. I promise.

Alan

Five games into the season, I now know the best soccer team that will win. Bill said that my knowledge of the game is superb and that I could win big if I backed my favourite team. I did initially dip my toe in the water and placed a small bet on a head-to-head win against the second ranked team. It came off as predicted. I did the same the next match. At work I kept boasting how good my skills were. I started to believe that this is where the money lay. I started to bet big but the next game, my team lost. I discounted this because two of the top players were off their game. I thought that I would double my bet in the following few games to catch up on my losses. I could hardly believe that the team is in a losing streak and

I am way behind. I keep boasting that I pick the winning team to my friends but I am way behind. I will double again next game and hope they will win, otherwise I will be in real strife with my mortgage payments.

Jim

1

What is gambling and when is it a problem or a disorder?

In time, many things change and many things remain the same. The Mirage Casino Hotel, Las Vegas, scene of my most recent conference presentation, and almost forty years since my first. There are new table card games on offer and the gaming machines that are resplendent with vibrant sounds, flashing lights and appealing sophisticated graphic designs. Yet the lure and attraction of the casino table games and electronic gaming machines still provokes the identical sense of excitement and desire to be in with the crowd and the action that was evident so many years ago. Let me reflect on that memorable first experience.

Atlantic City, early 1980s, Bally's Park Casino Hotel: the venue for my first international conference on gambling and risk-taking. It was also my first exposure to a casino. I hurried through hotel registration, deposited my luggage in my room, tipped the bellboy and with excited anticipation headed for the gambling floor. The cascade of noise, lights and movement of people all added to the dazzling atmosphere. Straight to the roulette table where I stood for several minutes watching others play and becoming familiar with the house rules. I took out the one hundred US dollars that I had set aside for gambling – the maximum I would allow myself to lose – and exchanged it for gambling chips. They were blue, I recall. The minimum stake was five dollars. Luck went my way, and after twenty minutes I was well in front. My urge satisfied, I left the table three hundred and sixty dollars richer. Tomorrow I would return and make more.

Early that next evening, several other delegates and I returned to the tables. Confident that my luck would continue, I chose the same roulette table and began playing. No win came. What was wrong, I asked, had they changed the wheel, was the croupier spinning the wheel differently? Soon the winnings from the day before had disappeared. I was down to my last twenty dollars of the allocated gambling kitty. My heart was pounding as I watched that last spin. I had to win. It didn't happen. I felt a surge of anger. It was directed toward me: why didn't I quit while I was in front? Now what would I do? I had lost not only my initial kitty but my winnings as well. I thought, 'I must draw out some more cash and try and win that money back. I'll stop once I win back the amount I lost, the amount that really belongs to me.'

I hastily retreated to the ATM machine conveniently located nearby, intent on taking out some of my holiday money to use to win my money back. But as I approached the machine I slowed down. Stop, I thought; I'm falling into the same pattern, the same trap, described by many of the gamblers I treat.

Let's deal with this situation sensibly, I said to myself. First, relax, slow down, reduce my level of arousal and feeling of agitation and pressure to obtain more money. Now, let's rethink the consequences of what I am doing. If I take my holiday money and lose that, how will I feel? Miserable and more angry at myself. And what will I do then? Take out more money to chase my losses? And if I lose that as well? Will I keep doing the same thing until I lose everything? If I have no money, then I will not be able to do what I had planned for my holidays. I will certainly be unhappy and remorseful.

I argued with myself. I could win, I insisted, my luck is bound to change.

Let's be realistic: gambling pushed me into this situation, more gambling won't get me out. My clients have taught me this through their own behaviour.

But the money I lost is rightfully mine; I should try to get it back.

Rubbish; the money I spent was for entertainment. I bought some excitement and enjoyment from the casino operators. The money is not mine, it's theirs. They provided me with an opportunity for fun, playing roulette, in exchange for payment. This is much the same thing as when I pay the box office for a ticket to enjoy myself at the cinema. If the show is bad, I don't go back to the ticket office and ask for my money back, do I? I accept that my money is gone. The same principle applies to gambling.

So I decided to learn from my clients' behaviour and avoid being trapped by the same pitfall. I relaxed and challenged my thoughts, considering the consequences of how I would feel when, not *if* but *when*, I lost again. Cut and accept my losses and do not create more problems; this was the proper approach.

It was not easy the next two days, watching others gamble and experiencing the urge to try my luck again. But applying what I had learnt about the process from my clients and the techniques described in this book, I resisted the impulse to return to the roulette. I lost my kitty as expected, but no more; and then, having returned home, went on to spend a most enjoyable few days holidaying in Hawaii.

Decades later, in Las Vegas, exactly the same process and decision-making were applied with exactly the same results; I had fun gambling what I could afford and intended to spend, and left for home with no regrets or guilt.

With help from this book you can overcome your gambling compulsion and raise the overall quality of your life by improving your financial position, your relationships with others and your ability to cope more effectively with pressure. The aim of this self-help guide is to help you regain control over your compulsive gambling habits by giving you a greater understanding of what gambling is and teaching you ways in which you can challenge and correct your distorted thoughts about gambling. It may not be easy, but remember: the results depend on the effort you put into helping yourself.

What is gambling?

Gambling is an attractive form of entertainment that most people have enjoyed at one time or other in their adult life at least on one or more occasions. In contemporary society, it is common for people to play cards for money with family members or school friends; to play bingo, fruit machines (electronic gaming machines found in arcades in the UK with no age restrictions) and other forms of gaming machines; to purchase lottery or raffle tickets or enter sweepstakes; and to bet off-track or visit casinos. Many of these activities can be either in land-based venues or through the Internet using computers, smartphones or tablets. All these activities are regarded as fun and are socially approved forms of leisure. Gambling in the company of friends, the possibility of winning and the gambling environment with its noise and lights all combine to make the experience attractive and exciting. Dreams of vast wealth and changes in fortune also entice people to try their luck: a jackpot could easily help pay off the mortgage, or mean an overseas holiday or a new car. However, most people are realistic: they hope to win, but really expect to lose. They only stake money that they can afford to lose. Although there may be a sense of disappointment at having lost, there is no concern about it by either the gambler or family members. It is apparent that the physical arousal generated by the prospect of winning is experienced as excitement and is the main factor attracting people to gambling.

What exactly is gambling and how do we distinguish it from other risk-taking activities? Perhaps the simplest explanation of what gambling is has been given by two American psychologists involved in the treatment of problem gamblers, D. W. Bolen and W. H. Boyd. They described gambling as 'the wager of any type of item or possession of value upon a game or event of uncertain outcome in which chance, of variable degree, determines such an outcome in order to obtain some gain/profit'.

We can say that there is general agreement that there are at least six essential components included in gambling:

1. Two or more parties are involved (one can be an organisation).
2. Events are based on uncertainty/chance.
3. Items of value are redistributed according to the outcome of those uncertain/chance events.
4. Items of value are not limited to money.
5. Participation is voluntary.
6. Participation is motivated by a desire to obtain a gain.

While the item of value that is staked is usually money, there have been cases in which people have bet possessions, property and even the sexual favours of their wives or daughters. According to one anecdote, a London police constable in the late 1800s chanced upon two shabbily dressed men in a quiet, foggy side street. One man was assisting the other, who appeared to the constable to be trying to hang himself from the lamppost. When he attempted to intervene and save the man from what he thought was suicide, the constable was told in no uncertain terms to go away and mind his own business. It transpired that one of the men was so sure that he had the winning hand in a game of cards that he bet his life he would win. Unfortunately, he lost and was now in the process of paying his debt.

Specifically excluded from the definition are activities that involve some degree of risk but do not include the transfer of items of value. This extends to such risk-taking behaviour as hang-gliding, crossing the road or driving fast – despite popular statements, for example, to the effect that 'the traffic is so heavy these days that it's a *gamble* trying to cross the road without being hit'. All gambling involves risk but not all risky behaviours involve gambling.

Gambling in society

There is nothing new about gambling, nor is it a peculiarly modern phenomenon. It is interesting to follow the development of gambling through the ages to shed some light on how society has reacted to problem gambling. Evidence exists to show that people have been gambling since ancient Egyptian times, 4000 years BC. Archaeological findings reveal that six-sided dice were used by the Etruscans and Romans around 900 BC and that in idle moments, Greek and Roman soldiers keenly wagered on the turn of numbered chariot wheels. This was the forerunner of roulette, a device refined by the French mathematician Blaise Pascal and introduced to England in 1739. It entered America in the nineteenth century and Australia as recently as 1973, where the game is now so popular that every Australian state and territory has one or more casinos.

Playing cards originated in twelfth-century China and reached Europe through Spain around the mid to late 1300s. Lotteries existed in early Roman days. Lots, that is the casting of numbers, were used by early courts in determining guilt, dividing property and electing politicians. Lotteries became popular as a means of raising funds for public projects. Queen Elizabeth I introduced lotteries to England in 1569 to finance public projects and the support of the poor. Lotteries raised funds for the American War of Independence: George Washington is reputed to have purchased the first ticket. According to an article by the Chicago crime commissioner Virgil Peterson, published in 1950, by 1790 'the lottery mania appear[ed] to rage with uncommon violence . . . Unscrupulous promoters incited the get rich mania among the people.' Horse racing, as John Day has noted, is 'a couple of thousand years older than Christianity'; Homer, Ovid and Herodotus were among the earliest of turf writers. Although public races were common in eleventh-century London, thoroughbred racing evolved from the horse-breeding inter-ests of King Henry VIII (1509–47). The sport gained status as a national pastime under King James I (1603–25), was suppressed only temporarily during Oliver Cromwell's reign and came to be formally regulated following the establish-ment of the Newmarket Jockey Club in 1750.

The poker machine, also known as the fruit or slot machine, was invented by the American Charles Frey in 1895 and has gained popularity as one of the most profitable gambling devices ever invented; as one anonymous writer put it, 'No other machine was ever invented from which profits derived were so fabulous on so small an investment, and with so little effort.' With technological advances, these machines have evolved into electronic gaming machines offering multiple games and the capacity to bet multiple credits on multiple lines. Graphics and sounds coupled with linked jackpots increase the entertainment and excitement value. It has now become the form of gambling that individuals in treatment report as contributing most to their problems.

Sociological and anthropological studies have shown that gambling is a near-ubiquitous phenomenon, found in almost every race and culture throughout history. The only exceptions are a few Native American and Australian aboriginal societies in which wealth is owned collectively rather than personally by individuals.

In Western society, socio-political forces have brought about a major change in attitudes toward gambling since the early decades of the twentieth century. In 1931, Nevada was the only state that permitted certain forms of gambling; now, with the exception of two, all states in the USA allow one or more forms. In England, the 1960 Betting and Gaming Act, which legalised off-course betting, ushered in a rise in gambling activity, a trend now clearly visible across Europe. Since the 1970s there has been unprecedented support for gambling as a legitimate form of community leisure activity, promoted by an extensive social, economic and political infrastructure.

Of significance, the advent of the Internet in the 1970s has led to a dramatic change in the gambling environment. What we have witnessed in the last four decades, and more so in the last, is not only the widespread use of communication globally, but also the degree to which it has become common in daily routines. Online shopping, banking, chatting, information gathering, emails and gaming are now commonplace activities. The implications for gambling are complex and pervasive. Individuals are now no longer restricted to land-based venues. Gambling is available 24/7 through a range of platforms including smartphones, tablets and laptops. National boundaries no longer exist in relation to gambling; someone in one country has ready access to regulated or unregulated online sites operating in other countries. It means effectively that anyone can gamble on virtually any form at any time they are inclined to place a bet.

The popularity of gambling is all the more interesting because of the absence of any obvious explanation of the drive to engage in this kind of behaviour in the form of an underlying biological need or a substance that could be seen to produce a physiological response, as in alcohol or drug use.

Heavy media promotion undoubtedly has an important influence on children and adolescents in encouraging them to see gambling as an exciting leisure activity. Advertising glamorises gambling and lures people into it by giving the misleading impression that winning is a routine event and that most players come out as winners.

One of the more pervasive influences has emerged in the context of sports betting. The options offered by online providers are now heavily marketed and advertised through the media to the extent where individuals can gamble not only the outcome of sporting events but those of elections and royalty naming a baby, to name but a few. Gambling-related advertising is often posted around sporting venues, odds offered by sporting commentaries during televised games and gaming logos of sponsorship companies prominently displayed on sports uniforms and related apparel. In this way, sports betting has become normalised, with under-aged children becoming heavily exposed to gambling, leading them to adopt the view that gambling is a standard and integral part of sports. This has been referred to as the 'gamblification of sports', and the 'sportification of gambling'. It should therefore come as no surprise that sports-betting activities represent a growing and increasingly lucrative industry. But the downside is that younger adults are now becoming more involved and consequently experiencing hardships.

While it is true to say that most people win on occasion, and that some of these wins may be large, the odds remain in favour of the house and invariably the vast majority of people lose in the long term. Even the gambling industry acknowledges that in all but the most unusual circumstances, individuals are guaranteed to lose the longer they play. Studies have shown that most gamblers almost always return their winnings through further gambling. There is a tendency not to be satisfied with the amount won, to believe that more money can be gained by continued gambling.

Exactly how many people participate in some form of gambling is determined by the availability and accessibility of gambling facilities. The greater the availability of gambling outlets, the greater the number of people who participate. And the greater number of people who participate, the greater the number of those who are placed at risk of developing a problem – of becoming what are popularly known as 'compulsive gamblers'. As gambling becomes more popular and new forms are introduced, increasing concern is being expressed by welfare organisations and by mental health professionals who recognise and deal with its darker side: the personal, social and economic impact of problem gambling. For example, the failing health of the 70-year-old who goes without food in order to have money to play the slot machines; or the pain of a family coping with the suicide of the father and the crisis of a ten-thousand-pound debt.

Before we look more closely at excessive and problem gambling, let us first pause and consider some of the terminology used to describe it, and some of the forms that gambling takes.

Terms used to describe problem gambling

To avoid confusion, it is important to differentiate the various terms commonly used of people who have lost control over their gambling behaviour.

Most people are probably most familiar with the term 'compulsive' gambling through its association with Gamblers Anonymous – a self-help group for people who experience recurrent uncontrollable urges to gamble. However, uncontrolled gambling has also been referred to as 'excessive', 'addictive', 'dependent', 'neurotic' and 'pathological'. More recently, use of 'gambling disorder' is becoming more common as a less pejorative label. Although used interchangeably, these terms do have important differences from a scientific point of view. For example, the popular description 'compulsive' is not really accurate when we consider the specific psychiatric definition of the word. In psychiatry, a compulsion refers to a persistent urge to carry out a behaviour that the person wishes to resist but is unable to because of high levels of anxiety and a fear that something bad will happen. It describes a condition known as obsessive–compulsive disorder in the broader class of anxiety disorders and is used to cover such behaviours as ritual hand-washing or repetitive checking. The person suffering the condition wishes to stop the behaviour because it is irrational and causes distress. The behaviour is motivated by a drive to reduce anxiety, and not for excitement or any positive gain.

This is not the case with 'compulsive' gamblers, who are, on the contrary, highly motivated to carry out their behaviour. They gain immense subjective excitement and arousal from gambling. The pressure to stop often comes from outside sources, in particular from people around them who recognise the financial ruin and personal distress caused by patterns of excessive gambling behaviour. This frequently puts the gambler in a position of conflict with those close to him or her. However, once you admit that gambling is causing problems either to yourself or to your loved ones, or both, then you are on the way to recovery.

In the mid–1970s, gambling entered into the medical arena as a recognised condition or disorder. In 1975, pathological gambling was included in the International Classification of Diseases, the international diagnostic system for categorising diseases, as a habitual behavioural disturbance. Then, in the early 1980s, largely through the efforts of the late Dr Robert Custer, an American psychiatrist, the term 'pathological gambling' came to be widely recognised and used in the field of mental health. Contributing to this was the inclusion of pathological gambling as an impulse control disorder in the American *Diagnostic and Statistical Manual of Mental Disorders* (DSM for short) in 1980. 'Pathological' is a medical term suggesting the presence of an underlying disease process. Its use in this context implied that pathological gambling was in some way a mental illness or disorder, with many features suggesting its equivalence to an impulse control disorder or to an addiction.

This disease model has been severely criticised, particularly by John Rosecrance, a professor of criminal justice who was tragically injured in a motor vehicle accident in outback Australia after presenting a seminal paper at a gambling conference, on the grounds that it unjustifiably medicalised a social behaviour. He and other clinicians have argued strongly that 'pathological' gambling is not a disease but a behaviour that falls on a continuum ranging from social and intermittent at one end through regular and heavy to excessive at the other: there is no real difference between the merely heavy and the 'pathological' gambler except for the amounts gambled. As a result, to get away from the medical disease model, many health professionals now prefer the neutral description of 'problem' gambling.

In the last two decades or so, clinical and neuroscience research has led to addiction as being the main model explaining why some people lose control over their behaviour. Firstly, it has been argued that there are similarities between gambling and substance-related addictions. The behaviour produces some excitement, arousal and/or changes in mood that is reinforcing and leads one to seek to repeat the response. With repetition, the behaviour becomes a habit but one that needs more and more intensity to produce the same effects – that is, tolerance to the behaviour or substance occurs. At the same time, stopping the behaviour or substance use leads to withdrawal symptoms that are unpleasant and eliminated only by resuming consumption. One primary characteristic is that the individual persists in consuming the behaviour or substance despite the serious negative consequences that emerge. Both in gambling and substance use, the negative consequences can be life-threatening for the former through depression and suicidality, and the latter, overdoses or physical illnesses.

Secondly, research in the domain of neuroscience has identified the role that brain chemicals (neurotransmitters) might play in making an individual likely to respond positively to behaviours or substances that alter mood states. Three neurotransmitters appear to be at work: serotonin, which influences impulsivity, norepinephrine or noradrenaline, which influences arousal, and dopamine, which affects mood and anticipation of rewards. Dopamine in particular has been linked to anticipation of rewards, cravings and urges similarly in gambling as in substance use. At the moment it remains unclear if the changes in brain chemistry represent a risk factor for developing addictive behaviours, or if they occur as the result of repeated excessive use.

In brief, the clinical findings that the causes, characteristics, clinical course, neurobiology and treatment of gambling disorders are similar in many respects to substance addiction have resulted in the condition being reclassified within the mental health field. In the latest edition of the American psychiatric diagnostic system (DSM-5, 2013), it has been relocated from the impulse-control to the substance-related and addictive category where it is subclassified as a non-substance behavioural addiction. 'Internet addiction' is another behaviour that is worthy of attention as a behavioural addiction but, as yet, has not been formally included alongside gambling disorder. Overall, this reclassification has consolidated the concept of gambling as an addiction.

Irrespective of brain chemistry being the cause or result of addiction, it is extremely important to avoid using brain chemistry as an excuse for failing to control behaviour. Brain chemistry does not control behaviour; that is the function of the frontal lobes of the brain that are involved in executive decision-making. One way to look at it with a common-sense view is to regard the brain chemistry as providing the drive or motivation to act in a certain way, whether to withdraw more money to gamble with, or to have another drink. The frontal lobe, however, is the captain steering the ship. It makes the final decision whether or not to follow a particular course of action.

Granted that it becomes more difficult to control urges when sitting in front of a gaming machine in a venue, or at the bar at a hotel, as compared to being a long distance from the venue. But, despite the strength of the urge, control over decision-making is still possible. What one cannot do is to continue making bad decisions using the excuse that 'I have no control over my behaviour because my brain chemistry made me do it.' This attitude leads to a defeatist position (or a justification to keep doing it) where one simply says, 'What is the point? I have an addiction, addiction is the disease, the addiction has control of my behaviour, therefore why fight it?'

All these terms have their limitations. However, for the purposes of this book we will use 'pathological' gambling, 'compulsive' gambling and gambling disorder in an equivalent sense to describe gamblers who display clear signs of impaired control, often popularly referred to as 'loss of control'. 'Problem' gambling is used to refer to the wider group of people who show some but not all signs of developing that condition. In this book we will concentrate on the group of people who are commonly described as compulsive gamblers. It is true that some compulsive gamblers are in reality heavy gamblers who have temporarily lost control. This distinction does not, however, affect the applicability of the step-by-step self-help guide in Part Two of this book, which can be used equally effectively by compulsive, problem and heavy gamblers alike.

Before we turn to the clinical features of compulsive gambling and how it may be overcome, we should first look at what it is about certain types of gambling that means they are more likely to cause problems.

The common forms of gambling

The mediums of gambling are almost limitless. People bet between themselves on the outcome of an event such as who will win the next football match, how many goals will be scored or who will score the first goal. These are informal agreements between participants with no set rules beyond those agreed to by them. In reality, the range of this type of gambling is limited only by the imagination of the players.

On a more formal level, organisations may operate certain games or activities within a framework of rules and regulations governing how the business will be conducted, often under national legislation or strict government guidelines, which are imposed to minimise cheating and crime and to ensure fair play. Casinos and off-track betting are good examples of gambling systems run in this way. Online forms of gambling offer new challenges and complexities for regulatory control given the ability of individuals to bypass restrictions within a country by accessing offshore sites.

Over the years many different activities have been regarded as 'gambling'. The list includes such pursuits as cards, dice, roulette and lotteries, as well as devices such as fruit or slot machines. You may be more surprised to learn that in the past even hobbies and sports such as tennis, walking and football were considered to be gambling mediums and were banned. Now, across the world organised betting takes place on the results of such disparate contests as elections and dog- and cock-fights, as well as on all major sporting events. Even promotional prizes offered by companies in pursuit of business and by retailers in shopping complexes constitute gambling.

Out of all this bewildering variety, four main categories of legal gambling can be identified: gaming, betting, lotteries and speculation.

- *Gaming* is the exchange of money on the outcome of a game. This category includes card games, fruit machines, video-draw poker machines, slot machines, two-up and casino games such as baccarat and roulette.
- *Betting* is staking money on the outcome of a future event. This category includes horse races (on the flat and over jumps), greyhound races, other sporting events and elections.
- *Lotteries* are the distribution of money by 'lot' or number, and include instant 'scratch' cards, raffles and bingo as well as lotteries themselves.
- *Speculation* is gambling on business, insurance or stock markets.

You may be puzzled to think that business and financial investments can also be regarded as gambling. Technically these activities meet the definition of gambling, but society has come to view them as falling within the bounds of economic activity. There are some grey areas such as day trading that can truly be considered gambling as the decision is based on the chance that a stock may rise or fall within a short time frame. In some cases, it might be worthwhile to accept day trading and stock-market investing as a form of gambling for anyone engaging in these activities to excess and for the wrong reasons. For these individuals, it may well be appropriate for them to obtain advice from an accountant or spouse or partner before placing trades, or having someone else manage the trades on their behalf. Many people now accept insurance as a means of protection and social security. Similarly with regard to business ventures and stock-market trading (but excluding trading in commodity futures and some other financial instruments), it is argued that outcomes are unpredictable, economic skills and sound business judgment are crucial elements brought to bear to minimise risk and maximise profits, and that far more than pure chance or luck is involved.

Which forms of gambling cause problems?

It should be clearly emphasised that not all forms of gambling lead to problems. Different levels of risk are associated with different types of gambling. Very few people experience impaired control over buying raffle tickets. There is a prolonged delay between the purchase of a ticket and its draw, and the draws are generally infrequent. On the other hand, many people suffer from slots, roulette, fruit-machine, horse-race or sports betting. Here, the delay between the 'purchase', that is, placing the bet, and knowing the outcome is very short, and the opportunity for further play is high; perhaps only a few seconds, several minutes or just a day or so.

It has been shown that those forms of gambling that readily lead to loss of control have two elements in common:

- the opportunity to place single large bets (as in horse-racing, sports betting or casinos) up to several thousand pounds; and/or
- the capacity for rapid continuous play bets where the interval between play is very short (a matter of seconds) and results are known, and pay-outs given, almost immediately (as in slots and fruit machines).

A further consideration is ease of access to gambling facilities. People are less likely to go to an off-course betting office or casino impulsively if it is located several miles away. The inconvenience of travel and/or parking vehicles is sufficient to cause them to reconsider the strength of their urge. This is precisely the reason why casinos in some countries require twenty-four hours' notice of intent to gamble or are located in non-metropolitan areas: the delay imposed between the decision to gamble and gaining access to the facilities allows would-be gamblers a period in which the urge can dissipate and they can reconsider their intent.

When in Cairo some time ago, for example, I attempted to enter a casino for research purposes, but I was barred from entry until I could produce my passport. To get it, I had to return to my hotel. On entering the casino I discovered that all wagers had to be made in US dollars; local currency was prohibited. By this stage, any interest in playing roulette had disappeared, because I could not be bothered with exchanging foreign currency. This strategy was directed at, and highly effective in, protecting local residents from gambling. Such restrictions are now less frequently found but in some jurisdictions players have to register before being able to enter the gaming floor in a casino. Similarly, the wife of a patient recently complained bitterly that her husband had shown no interest in gambling until electronic gaming machines were approved in a local hotel within walking distance of their home. In the space of three months he had lost seven hundred pounds and had become irritable and distant, a changed personality. Despite her repeated protestations, he continued to gamble in the vain hope of recovering the amounts he had already lost. He had begun chasing losses.

Accessibility is important in terms of time as well as location. Facilities that are open from early morning until late at night can cater to a wider range of clients, including those working shifts as well as those with regular work hours. Online gambling now offers the convenience of placing bets at any time from any location using smartphones or tablets, and from the convenience of home, office or travelling.

Gambling in excess

It has long been acknowledged that excessive gambling produces social and economic costs: poverty, starvation, family disintegration and criminal behaviour. One of the first reported cases refers to an ancient Egyptian who was condemned to slavery in the salt mines for gambling to excess. Aristotle criticised gamblers, and the Jews debarred them from holding public office or appearing as witnesses because of their characteristic flaws and untrustworthiness. Religious attitudes varied, but some condemned gambling outright. The Qur'an forbade it, and eleventh-century Christian clergy were admonished for retarding the spread of the Church through their encouragement of gambling.

Gambling was not of itself illegal under English common law, but various Acts of Parliament were introduced to lessen breaches of peace and public order, corruption and cheating. Similar concerns are often expressed today about the relationship between gambling and organised crime, money laundering and cheating. Statutes of Richard II (1388), Edward IV (1477) and Henry VIII (1541) legislated against gambling in order to prevent impoverishment among soldiers, and to promote archery practice and military preparedness by eliminating the practice of gambling weapons.

In England and France alike, the negative impact of excessive gambling led to the government taking action to curb or restrict the practice. Severe penalties were imposed; for example, the criminal offence of vagrancy was extended to cover illegal gamblers who, for repeated offences, were branded, enslaved or executed. America responded to issues of family welfare, public safety and juvenile delinquency with the enactment of anti-gambling legislation in the mid-1700s.

Concerns similar to those expressed today by welfare organisations stemmed from the realisation that the problem was widespread within the community. Severe loss and tragic consequences were common. Among the many famous historical figures who reputedly either manifested signs of excessive gambling or who had ruin brought upon them are Lord Halifax, Lord Shaftesbury, Voltaire, Horace Walpole, Marie Antoinette and Nell Gwyn. The historian John Ashton in 1898 observed that the 'number of great men who played heavily, the number of fortunes wrecked at this time is almost incredible', and cited as illustrative examples the cases of Charles James Fox, Lord Carlisle and the Duke of Wellington, who had to sell his commission to clear his gambling debts. The same comment could be made today, with a number of sports figures, celebrities and leading business identities losing vast sums due to their gambling. A prominent lawyer in Australia was recently imprisoned for embezzling in excess of a million dollars from his trust funds to support his gambling.

The compulsion to gamble is well described by the historian Clemens France, who wrote in 1902 that many gamblers

in their desperation strip themselves on the spot of their clothes, either to stake against money or to pledge the keeper of the table for a trifle to renew their play, and many instances occur of men going home half naked, having lost their all . . . The passion for gambling gives no time for breathing; it is an enemy which gives neither quarter nor truce; it is a persecutor, furious and indefatigable.

Consider the similarity of France's description with that of an email I received from a compulsive gambler in 2016:

I have been gambling for the last nine years at the casino, mainly table games of roulette and baccarat. I also spend time on the machines when I want to just get away from things. Some bad decisions during this time have led to large losses, and in desperation, led me to do a few things that I regret. What I did caused me to appear before the courts on no less than four occasions. I have been homeless many times and my life has become unmanageable. When I am gambling, I do not think of the consequences, I don't care about anything else. I have readily blown my rent and food money to have that one more chance to win. It doesn't worry me. My second wife has left with the two children, both under three years of age. Even so, all I can dream of is the big win which will turn my life around for the better.

In 1817, lotteries were prolific but, according to France, the 'depression and excitement that so invariably followed the drawings diverted the labourer from his work, weakened his moral tone, consumed his earnings and soon brought pauperism'. By 1882 virtually every European state prohibited gambling.

Historically, the primary aim of anti-gambling legislation has been the social protection of community members. Certain activities, although inherently enjoyable in their own right, are seen to need restriction because of their deleterious effect and cost to the community as a whole. Yet people voluntarily pursue the opportunity to gamble, despite efforts to prevent them doing so, because most see gambling as an essentially exciting leisure pursuit and as offering a prospect of quick and easy wealth. Moreover, many governments see it as a lucrative source of revenue, and are consequently reluctant to limit it too far.

For some people, the urge to gamble is so persistent and excessive that it causes severe interference to many aspects of their own life, as well as to the lives of their spouses or partners and family members. To gain a better understanding of the strong psychological forces acting upon you, the gambler, I recommend reading some of the descriptions contained in classical works of literature such as Pushkin's 'The Queen of Spades', Thackeray's 'A Gambler's Death', Saki's 'The Stake' and Dostoevsky's *The Gambler*. Dostoevsky's description of the irresistible urge is based upon his personal experience, for he himself was, as P. Squires has described, 'powerless in the clutches of his terrific gambling mania, which blunted his sense of moral responsibility as effectively as extreme alcohol addiction could'. These works describe the powerful grip of gambling, and the thought processes that lead to one making very poor decisions. They are well worth reading to gain an insight into how emotions and urges can result in poor decisions.

We know that the majority of people who gamble to excess develop psychological symptoms of depression and anxiety; many turn to alcohol or drugs as a means of temporarily escaping their problems. In some cases, the stress of financial pressures may even be so strong as to lead the person to commit a crime in order to cover his debts or provide money with which to continue gambling. The attempt is made to conceal debts and avoid others finding out the full extent of their difficulties and behaviours. The fear of discovery and its repercussions strains the already-fragile emotional state of the gambler, causing him or her to withdraw from social and family life; partnerships and marriage relationships deteriorate dramatically. The emotional turmoil interferes with concentration and the ability to perform properly at work, increasing the risk of being sacked. In a large minority of cases, guilt and remorse combined with agitation, fear of discovery and the concomitant intense public embarrassment and humiliation can lead to serious suicide thoughts. These thoughts are commonly experienced and, in a few, can result in attempts being made. Unfortunately, some do succeed, research showing around ten or more individuals per year in Western countries. Where someone does experience suicidal thoughts, be aware that proper care and management can be offered to reduce the likelihood of self-harm and, with support from those around, the process of recovery can be begun.

But if you do have a gambling problem, do not despair; the cycle can be broken and recovery achieved. Remember: no matter how bleak the outlook appears, you can regain command of the situation and work toward personal development and self-improvement. With appropriate help, your partnership or marriage can be improved, performance at work stabilised and stresses reduced. Compulsive gambling is treatable and many do overcome its grip. In fact, evidence indicates that 65 to 85 per cent of problem gamblers do recover. This book is designed to be of assistance to this group of individuals in helping them regain control over their behaviour and emotions and improve their quality of life, not to mention that of their families and those around them.

I can remember exactly when my problem started. I was sixteen years of age. My friends and I managed to bluff our way into the bar for a few drinks. We started to play the fruit machines and after about half an hour I won what was a large amount of money to me, thirty dollars. I was so excited, my heart was racing and the fact that I had won made me feel so special. I thought, this is easy money. The next day I looked forward to returning to win more. I couldn't stop. Soon my friends were annoyed at my always wanting to go to the bar instead of the movies or to parties. I avoided them and gambled alone. Then once I lost more than I really could afford, I got angry; I had to win my money back. I kept going back. After a while my debts were so great that more gambling was the only way out. I became really depressed, but what angered me most was the lies I told to cover up what I was doing . . . But still I couldn't stop. The change came when I admitted my problem to my parents. They helped me to open up, to communicate with others and to deal with each problem I had created. They gave me hope. Through their efforts, my self-esteem and confidence grew. I owe them a lot.

John

What are the characteristics of problem gambling?

Most people gamble sensibly within their financial means, but for a few gambling is an over-riding passion that dominates many aspects of their life. They become obsessed with the anticipation of the next bet, playing electronic gaming machines or joining a card game, and so become preoccupied with thoughts of where to get more money so that they can carry on gambling. In these cases, the gambler is transformed into a withdrawn and moody person who is constantly plagued by worries about meeting debt repayments, finding daily living expenses and concealing debts.

These are the people for whom this book is written: those who are said to be compulsive or problem gamblers. For them, the urge to gamble is difficult to control or manage, and as a result has a major impact on personal, family and work activities. Take Mary, a 45-year-old mother of two grown-up daughters. The children have now left home and she is on her own during the day, bored and lonely. Her advertising executive husband works late hours. She has developed a habit of going to bingo virtually every day; here she can play bingo or spend time on gaming machines, allowing her to forget about her hassles and disappear into a world of her own. The problem is that she is losing all her money, skimping on food and clothing purchases to have enough to go on playing. She has dreams of bingo almost every night and can hardly wait until her husband leaves for work in the morning so she can go to the bingo hall, where she spends most of the day. She neglects her appearance and the home, much to the confusion of her husband, who is unaware of what she is doing.

The compulsion is so strong that it appears to be beyond control. It may come on suddenly or after exposure to a particular cue or stimulus, for example, reading the lottery or race results in a newspaper. Once the thought of gambling enters the person's mind, it grows in strength to the extent that all concentration is directed toward finding ways of satisfying it as quickly as possible. In some instances, having begun gambling the person is totally possessed by the urge to the point where he or she may not be able to stop, even though they may need to return home or to work. John, an electrician by trade, would often remain at the pub playing machines instead of returning to work. Just another few goes on the machine, he would tell himself, before I go back just in case I hit the jackpot. The more the gambler is in debt and needs to win, the greater is the compulsion to return again and again.

Joanne is a 54-year-old housewife whose thoughts about playing the lottery have taken over her whole life. Every night she goes to sleep dreaming of winning the lottery, fantasising how she would spend her money: pay off the kids' mortgages, travel to Barcelona, furnish her home the way she would like – new curtains, a new kitchen and carpets. She skimps on household spending just to get a few more pence for another ticket. It is a ritual each time a draw is to be televised. Each morning, she wakes excited, almost unable to wait to watch the television; she will never go out just in case she misses the show. Her husband is fed up with her constant preoccupation with the lottery, her lack of interest in the marriage and their home, and the couple are now slowly drifting apart.

People who compulsively gamble to excess commonly report the following feelings.

Before gambling:

- An increasing preoccupation with gambling, to the point where nothing else is important. This is often experienced as a sense of 'craving'.
- A fear that they may miss an opportunity to win. How many times have we heard of the unhappy person whose lucky numbers turned up but who had forgotten to buy their ticket, or stopped playing the gaming machines only to have the next person win the jackpot?

- Irrational confidence and fantasies about winning.
- Excitement in anticipation of buying the 'winning' ticket, hitting the jackpot or the horse coming first. Fantasising what to do with the winnings.
- Irritation, anger and mounting tension if something prevents them from gambling.

During gambling:

- A total focus of attention on gambling; all else fades in importance.
- Excitement and physical arousal, shown by increased heart rate.
- Irrational talk inside their head: the next bet is the winner I have been waiting for. It must be my turn soon for a large win, I just know it.
- Superstitious behaviour to increase the chance of a win.

After a successful session:

> - Relief and anticipation of the next occasion.
> - Confidence (I knew I could do it) and a conviction that winning was a result of skill.
> - Elated mood.
> - Inflated ego, having beaten 'them' at their own game.
> - Self-satisfaction at having money and being able to impress a partner or spouse.

After losing:

> - Guilt and remorse.
> - Fear of spouse or others finding out.
> - Worry over where to obtain money to cover living expenses.
> - Thoughts of what lies to tell to cover one's actions.
> - Self-directed anger.
> - Determination never to gamble again – but at the same time, thoughts of where to find money in order to return to chase losses.
> - Desire to forget problems through alcohol.

One question often asked is whether there is a 'gambling-prone personality'. The answer is simple and straight-forward: there is *no* such gambling personality type. Furthermore, there is *no* individual personality trait that is commonly to be found in gamblers. Gamblers include all types of personality, and all kinds of personality traits are found in gamblers.

There are nevertheless general signs that partners and family members can look out for as signals that a problem might exist. These are:

- lengthy or unexplained times away from work and home;
- complaints of poor productivity at work;
- betting tickets suggesting large bets;
- preferring to play slot machines alone instead of remaining in social company at pub or club;
- always being short of cash despite regular income;
- having a number of credit cards with little available credit;
- having multiple loans;
- mood shifts coinciding with major race meeting days;
- spending excessive time on the Internet playing card or casino-type games;
- preoccupation with studying the form guide, listening to races or watching race broadcasts;

- friends who comment on the amount of money borrowed from them;
- calls from creditors requesting payment for out-standing debts, or threats of legal action;
- sudden job changes;
- repeated bounced cheques;
- monies or items disappearing from the home;
- discovering less money in bank accounts than should be there.

For the individual gambler, a good self-assessment is obtained by answering honestly the twenty questions listed by Gamblers Anonymous. These are:

1. Did you ever lose time from work due to gambling?
2. Has gambling ever made your home life unhappy?
3. Did gambling affect your reputation?
4. Have you ever felt remorse after gambling?
5. Did you ever gamble to get money with which to pay debts or otherwise solve financial difficulties?
6. Did gambling cause a decrease in your ambition or efficiency?
7. After losing, did you feel you must return as soon as possible and win back your losses?
8. After a win, did you have a strong urge to return and win more?
9. Did you often gamble until your last dollar was gone?

10. Did you ever borrow to finance your gambling?
11. Have you ever sold any real property (i.e. assets such as shares, real estates, non-personal items) or personal property to finance gambling?
12. Were you reluctant to use 'gambling money' for normal expenditures?
13. Did gambling make you careless of the welfare of your family?
14. Did you ever gamble longer than you had planned?
15. Have you ever gambled to escape worry or trouble?
16. Have you ever committed, or considered committing, an illegal act to finance gambling?
17. Did gambling cause you to have difficulty in sleeping?
18. Do arguments, disappointments or frustrations create within you an urge to gamble?
19. Did you ever have an urge to celebrate any good fortune by a few hours of gambling?
20. Have you ever considered self-destruction as a result of your gambling?

Some of the best predictors of pathological gambling are:

- the compulsion to chase losses;
- repeated failed efforts to stop gambling; and
- gambling in response to negative emotions such as stress and depression.

Despite the fact that gambling has led to the development of serious financial problems, compulsive gamblers hold a firm but wrong belief that more gambling is the solution to their troubles, that a win will save them by allowing them to pay off the debt. However, the cycle can be broken. With the help of this book, you can learn to identify the errors in your thinking. Once you understand the various steps down the path to problem gambling, you can reverse the process and change your behaviour for the better.

2

How does the problem develop?

Most gamesters begin at small games; and, by degrees, if their money or estates hold out, they rise to great sums; some have played first all their money, then their rings, coach or horses, even their wearing clothes and perukes; and then such a farm; and, at last, perhaps a lordship.

(From The Nicker Nicked, published in 1619)

Usually, problems generated by gambling emerge gradually over a period of time. Some do so almost immediately as soon as they began gambling. Many people are unable to recognise the exact point at which they lost control. All they are aware of is a steady progressive worsening of their financial situation and finding themselves needing to spend more time and money gambling and lying to others to cover up their behaviour. Like many alcoholics, they do not see the problem for what it is until they are right in the middle of a crisis and when others complain about their actions. Even then, many will deny that there is anything wrong and react with anger and resentment at any suggestion that there is a problem. These people are in denial, or do not want to confront the reality of needing to stop because of their mistaken belief that further gambling can resolve their financial woes. Distortions in their thinking enable them to minimise the depth of their predicament or rationalise away their behaviour, saying that this is only a temporary situation caused by some bad luck. They firmly hold the expectation that improvement is just around the corner.

The process leading to compulsive gambling is simple, but the pattern varies. Initially, people gamble at acceptable levels of expenditure, that is, only risking amounts that they can afford. However, at some point in time and often for reasons that are not entirely clear, control is lost. The loss of control may take one of two forms: an inability to resist an opportunity to gamble, or an inability to cease gambling once it has started.

Looking back on it, I don't really know when it became a problem. All I know is that I found myself drawn back to the machines. I couldn't stop thinking about them. They had a magic that enchanted me and I spent more and more time playing. Gradually all my money, I mean all my money, was used to play those wretched machines. I felt really angry having to pay bills because it meant I had less to play with.

Mary

At other times, loss of control may happen rapidly, the excitement of winning on the first few occasions being so profound that the person becomes addicted almost instantaneously. Early wins are also important in setting up the false expectations that one can make 'easy' money through gambling. Around three-quarters of gamblers say that a large win in the early stages of their career led them to believe that gambling was an easy way of supplementing their income.

In other cases, the decline is gradual but progressive. Some individuals find that after many years of controlled behaviour, the frequency and intensity of their gambling increase. They may sometimes gamble for longer and lose more money than they intended. Then, in the hope of making good their losses, they return to try their luck again, aiming to win to break even. This is the first step into the 'chasing cycle', a process well described by the American sociologist Professor Henry Lesieur in his book *The Chase*. The more gamblers try to recoup their losses, says Lesieur, the deeper they plunge into debt and the more pressure is exerted on them to return to repeat the cycle. So it goes on until they find themselves in a hopeless financial position.

Finally, as in alcoholism, some go on to gamble in binges. A binge is a sudden prolonged session or bout of excessive gambling. The main feature is a burst of frenetic gambling coupled with a subjective sense of impaired control where the person feels he or she just cannot stop. No consideration is given to what the final outcome will be. There is a sense of desperation and self-destructiveness as the gambler loses vast amounts over relatively short periods. The interval between sessions may vary in length from several weeks to many months, and is characterised by periods of remorse and minimal or no urge to gamble.

The phases of a compulsive gambling disorder

Clinicians have identified three phases through which most problem gamblers pass in their career, although how quickly they pass through each phase, as I have mentioned, varies substantially. These are:

- the winning phase;
- the losing phase;
- the desperation phase.

The winning phase

We all have to start somewhere. In the winning phase, a person is introduced to some form of gambling, quite often by parents or friends. The idea is to have fun, so one quickly learns that gambling is associated with action and excitement. This excitement might be produced by the thrill of winning, enjoying some aspect of the gambling environment in the company of friends, or forgetting life's daily hassles and problems, at least for a little while. As mentioned, about three-quarters of compulsive gamblers report that they had a 'large' win some time shortly after they first began. The win does not have to be large in absolute terms, only in relation to one's income. To a twelve-year-old, a ten-pound win may represent a large amount. John was a boy of fourteen when his father gave him a scratch card. He remembers slowly scratching the card to reveal the right numbers to win two pounds. He wanted another, and soon another. It is worth remembering that the average age at which a person starts to gamble is around twelve to fifteen years of age, although with females it tends to be older, with some not beginning until their early thirties; and it is usually parents, grandparents or friends who introduce an adolescent to gambling.

Winning leads to fantasies about winning more and an attitude that gambling is an easy and quick way of 'earning' additional income. Early wins, the 'beginner's luck' – perhaps more appropriately called 'beginner's *bad* luck' for some – give the novice gambler a sense of undue confidence in the ability to win and a strong belief in continued luck.

The losing phase

Unfortunately, we all know that luck does not hold out. The longer one gambles, the greater is the likelihood of losing. How many times have we heard someone complain that they won several pounds the first time they tried gambling but since then, they have lost it all and more besides. Peter, a plumber, was ecstatic when he won two hundred pounds on the slot machines during a work Christmas party at the club. He was the centre of attention, all his mates were talking about his luck. He felt good. He just had to return to play some more. He persuaded his friends to come with him because he wanted to impress them with his luck again. His ego-trip gave way to disappointment when he lost half his original winnings. Embarrassed and angry at himself, he went back by himself now, just to recover the amount lost. But he kept losing. As his losses grew, he became more and more emotionally distressed.

Eventually one loses more than one intends or can afford, and then attempts to recover by 'chasing' losses, that is, pouring more and more money into gambling with the hope of winning amounts already lost, as Peter had done. The unpredictability of the outcome, with wins coming every so often, reinforces this hope and encourages the chasing process. But repeated losses pull the gambler further and further behind and into debt, until he is prepared to take even greater risks in an increasingly desperate pursuit of the big win that will get him back to square one. The gambler begins secretive gambling, seeking sources of more money to gamble with, covering up losses and lying, losing time from work, borrowing from financial institutions, neglecting home life and failing to pay debts, and becoming increasingly emotionally distressed.

The desperation phase

Soon the gambler is plunged into the desperation phase, caught up in a cycle of chasing losses, winning occasionally, then suffering more losses and so on in a tightening downward spiral. Irrational gambling begins. The frequency and size of bets increase and bigger debts are accumulated until rock bottom is reached. Everything else is neglected – work, family relationships and social life. At this point the gambler is out of control. Nothing matters except finding more money to gamble, even to the point where many will begin to steal or embezzle funds to support their habit.

Lee, an ambitious 22-year-old bank teller, was given a tip by a customer for a good bet on an upcoming horse race. Lee was impressed because this customer frequently deposited large amounts, claiming that they were betting wins. He withdrew a hundred pounds from one of his customers' accounts, with the intention of using this to place his bet and returning it first thing in the morning before anyone could trace the transaction. He won. But then he repeated the process a few more times after being given further tips by his customer. Then came the fateful day when he lost heavily. He did not have enough money the following morning to cover up his transaction. So he carried out a transfer of funds from another account. The following day he lost again. Now he was transferring funds across two separate customer accounts. At this point, he should have recognised the danger signals and taken steps to discuss the matter with his wife and manager. It was still possible to minimise the damage. But he failed to act sensibly. Within twelve months he was seventy thousand pounds in debt, all of it embezzled from customers' accounts. Each morning he would be the first to arrive at work, feverishly transferring funds in an ever-increasing chain to avoid detection. After the stress of work he would go to the local bar each afternoon and drink to seek relief.

How was his deception discovered? His manager insisted that he take his annual leave. He refused, but to no avail. He knew what would happen. On the very first day of his absence, the replacement teller noted a discrepancy in one account of fifty pounds and informed the manager. The auditors were called, and by the week's end, Lee was facing a charge of fraud. The magistrate, recognising his compulsive gambling habit, imposed a four-year jail term. His wife, left with a one-year-old daughter, was shattered. He had some luck left, though: his wife was supportive and was prepared to wait for his release.

Lee's is not an isolated case. Studies have shown that 60 per cent of compulsive gamblers commit a non-violent property crime such as theft, passing dud cheques, shoplifting, embezzlement or misappropriating company funds. In about 20 per cent of these cases, the gambler is caught and charged, sometimes incurring a sentence of imprisonment. For example, one legal secretary regularly took small amounts out of her petty cash system to play the slot machines during her lunch break. She became panicky when she was about one hundred pounds behind, and tried to win the money back by spending more time at the machines. Eventually she accumulated a loss of three thousand pounds. She could not afford to repay this amount from her weekly salary, so her only option seemed to be to continue gambling so that she could win enough to replace her losses and escape detection. Eighteen months later, a routine company audit uncovered a shortfall of eleven thousand pounds. She was charged, convicted and sentenced to six months in prison. Her husband and eight-year-old daughter were devastated.

These, admittedly, are among the more serious cases, but most gamblers commit acts that make them feel miserable within themselves, for example, stealing small amounts from a spouse or partner, or from the purses or wallets of friends, stealing items from work or forging signatures on cheques.

For people early on in their compulsive gambling career, this book can prevent the decline into the desperation phase, while for those already there, it provides an effective strategy to begin the process of recovery. If there is one message to be learnt from this book, it is this. Gambling, no matter what form, is constructed in such a way that, mathematically, the chances of winning are stacked against the player. In all but the most exceptional of cases, the longer you keep playing, the more you are guaranteed to lose. It is the operator not you who will profit financially from your gambling.

3

Who is at risk of being affected?

Many people gamble, but only a relatively small percentage lose control and suffer problems as a result. Therefore, it seems that not everyone is at risk of developing compulsive gambling habits. Research has established some general guidelines for use in highlighting those individuals who may be particularly at risk. In this chapter we shall consider some of the more clearly identified factors that contribute to a high risk, before going on to set out three major paths of entry into problem gambling.

Risk factors

Income is an obvious and important starting point. Findings have consistently shown that people on low incomes and unemployed persons are vulnerable to gambling problems. Low earners have less disposable income available to spend on leisure pursuits than those who earn high salaries. As a result, problems emerge at a much earlier stage in proceedings and tend to persist over a longer period, because of the wage-earner's limited resources and restricted access to financial assistance. For example, consider two individuals, one with fifty pounds of disposable income a fortnight and the other with two hundred pounds. Assume both spend twenty pounds gambling. For one, this represents 40 per cent of his income; for the other, 10 per cent. Should both establish a debt of five hundred pounds and begin to pay it back at the same rate of forty pounds a week, the person on the lower income will struggle to meet the repayments, thus immediately facing the temptation to gamble more in order to try to ease the financial pressure. In addition, the person on the lower income is likely to find it much more difficult to borrow funds. In these circumstances, there is a greater risk of the person turning to illegal means to obtain money to supplement living expenses.

Age, gender and gambling medium are other risk factors which interact with one another. Young males between the ages of sixteen and thirty playing fruit and slot machines and betting on horse races are more at risk than their contemporaries purchasing weekly lottery tickets. In addition, this age group is more technically savvy and have access to smartphones, laptops and tablets, allowing them to easily and readily access the Internet at any time and any place to gamble. Bingo and instant scratch cards have greater appeal for older females, although evidence is showing that many more are turning to the Internet to gamble. There is some anecdotal evidence, according to David Miers, professor of law at Cardiff Law School, that scratch cards are more popular with working-class females, for whom betting in off-course betting offices is socially difficult, and mothers caring for children, who can easily purchase tickets during shopping trips.

The feature perhaps most consistently associated with problem gambling is impulsivity. Problem gamblers manifesting impulsivity show a tendency to have commenced gambling at an earlier age, spend more money gambling and display greater levels of financial difficulty than non-impulsive gamblers. They also show greater disturbances in other areas of their life: unstable work histories, poor interpersonal relationships and substance abuse.

As mentioned already, there is no known personality profile associated with an increased risk of impaired control over gambling. A number of studies have suggested that gamblers recorded higher scores on psychometric measures of depression, poor tolerance for boredom, addiction and anti-social personality, but it remains unclear whether these contribute to loss of control or are the end result of stress caused by the need to deal with problems generated by gambling. Nor is there any link between 'sensation-seeking' and gambling. On the contrary, studies have repeatedly shown that problem gamblers as a group achieved lower scores on such measures than members of the general population.

Perhaps the best way of seeing who is at risk is to look at the various pathways leading to the development of problem gambling.

An integrated model of problem gambling

There is a growing recognition that problem gambling is

not a unitary disorder but affects several subtypes of people who share several features in common. I have proposed an integrated model that postulates three major entry pathways into problem gambling. Let us examine these in detail, because this will enable us to appreciate the multiple factors that act in combination to produce impaired control in gamblers. The first point to make is that cultural and social attitudes held by a society will dictate the extent to which gambling is an accepted recreational activity. Some cultures regard gambling as morally wrong and prohibit it, often on the basis of religious values and teachings; others hold a more liberal perspective and allow certain forms but regulate it through government legislation.

Pathway one: The 'normal' or 'behaviourally conditioned' problem gambler

This first pathway is linked to the environment and learning. Environment is important in providing both the opportunity to gamble in the first place, and the advertising that glamorises and actively promotes participation. Early large wins, intermittent winning and the excitement of the gambling environment combine to establish a gambling habit. At the same time, specific beliefs and attitudes are firmly set down; these include the notion that winning is possible, that one has above-average skills or is able to influence the outcome during play, that luck is with or will soon come to one, and a tendency to dismiss losses in preference to concentrating on wins.

At some point, more money than originally intended is lost and the gambler begins to chase losses through further gambling. A habit emerges that is difficult to break, its continuance constantly encouraged by financial pressures.

People in this group do not necessarily have pre-existing psychological problems. Although they may show symptoms of depression, anxiety and substance abuse, these are emotional reactions that are secondary to the problems generated by gambling. Entry down this path may occur at any age in either gender, and may be triggered by exposure to gambling through the influence of chance, family members or friends. The intensity of gambling and the severity of the problems produced are lower for these gamblers than for those in the other groups. These gamblers have more insight into their problems, are more motivated to seek treatment of their own accord, are more likely to comply with treatment instructions and respond much better in terms of outcome. Individuals in this category are more likely to be able to resume controlled levels of gambling after treatment. If you are in this category, with the help of this book you have a very good chance of recovery.

Pathway two: The psychologically or emotionally vulnerable gambler

Some people have difficulty managing stress or dealing with crisis situations. They may suffer from depression or anxiety and use methods that allow them to escape problems rather than confronting them directly. Lack of ability to cope with stress and deal with problems may have been caused by past traumas, child abuse, disturbed family upbringing or inadequate role models. These individuals may be suffering feelings of insecurity, low self-esteem and a sense of rejection. They develop feelings of personal unhappiness, low mood, anxiety and tension. For them gambling becomes a means of emotional escapism, a means by which they can forget their problems through the distraction of excitement.

Often in these circumstances, a person becomes so absorbed in an activity that they enter what is called a state of dissociation. Dissociation is an alteration and distortion in perception that allows a person to split off and forget unpleasant emotions. They become totally absorbed with the activity; it becomes their full focus of attention. A good example of dissociation or absorption in everyday experience is that of driving. You can no doubt recall a time when you were so preoccupied with thoughts that you may have driven several miles without being consciously aware of what you were doing. You were driving safely, only you didn't register your actions in consciousness. It was an automatic habit that you carried out. Similarly, in one case I saw recently, Allan would spend three or four hours playing the gaming machines, but he could not remember how he got to the club or what he was doing during all that time. He said that he could remember suddenly being at the club, heading toward the machines, and then nothing until he was leaving the premises. His sense of time perception was dramatically altered; he would swear that he only spent less than half an hour gambling.

In this category we can identify a number of subgroups of gamblers, all in some circumstance of personal stress. We have the young male whose life ambitions are being frustrated. He has not achieved his ambitions at work; he sees his friends getting further and further in front of him in respect of marriage and career advancement, and enjoying the benefits of a home, car and holidays. The gambler feels left behind, resentful and disillusioned. Problems at work are often taken home, creating family and partnership conflicts. In response and to escape home and work stress, the gambler finds satisfaction in gambling.

For some women, the stress of an unhappy relationship, disappointments, a failing marriage, loneliness or boredom with their life is sufficient to tip the balance over toward excessive gambling. They avoid succumbing to depression by immersing themselves in gambling. They see little future for themselves, trapped in unhappy circumstances from which they see no prospect of escape. Women tend to gamble at a later age in life than males, around forty to fifty. In a handful of cases, I have noted that women in conflict with their husbands, or who discover their husbands having affairs, will gamble excessively in an unconscious act of aggression directed at 'getting even' with their husbands by spending all their savings. Fortunately, women show a more positive attitude toward treatment and seek help much earlier than males.

For gamblers who are vulnerable, any stress, no matter what its source, can be sufficient to push them over the edge into compulsive gambling. Even positive events can have this effect. Several gamblers have said that they have gone on a gambling binge following the birth of a baby. Whether they felt rejected, reacted against all the attention being directed toward the baby, or were fearful of losing their wife's affection is uncertain; what we do know is that they have embarked on a chaotic episode of severe gambling over a short period.

If you find yourself in any one of these categories, be aware that your gambling will show a tendency to escalate during periods of stress or crisis. For you, abstinence is perhaps the best goal of treatment. In addition to the approaches described in this book, the techniques outlined in the self-help book in this series on dealing with panic and anxiety, *Overcoming Anxiety* by Helen Kennerley, will be very useful in helping you cope with stress and its effects on gambling.

Pathway three: The biologically based or impulsive gambler

There is a small group of gamblers who show signs of a wide range of impulsive behaviours from early childhood onwards. These people have often had problems with learning, concentration and attention at school; they find themselves being overactive and needing a lot of stimulation, becoming bored very easily, and like to get involved in new activities; they tend to do things on impulse without thinking about the consequences of their actions. They are more likely to experiment with alcohol and drugs from an early age and to have difficulty holding down a job for any length of time because they lose interest in what they are doing; they generally do not have any long-term commitment or ambition in life. For these people, gambling starts at a much earlier age in childhood and can lead rapidly to serious financial trouble. Quite often the gambling occurs in binges, with the additional danger that they also become very depressed and begin drinking to excess, also in binges. This combination increases the risk of self-harm.

John was an intelligent 25-year-old spray painter who managed to get through school without doing much work. He was constantly in trouble for acting silly in class, much preferring to be out and about – he was involved in many different active sports – and as an adolescent was always in the thick of things, down at the clubs and bars or driving around on his motorcycle, frequently drinking too much and experimenting with a wide variety of soft drugs. From an early age he used to like betting on anything, even on a dare. He was never interested in hard work. He managed to find jobs easily because of his outward nature, pleasant personality and intelligence, but would never stay in one for more than six to twelve months. Once he was familiar with his work, he became bored and restless, and then turned to gambling and socialising instead. In his early twenties, he became more and more dissatisfied and depressed because he did not seem to be getting on in life. Fortunately, his girlfriend encouraged him to see a counsellor who taught him some of the techniques outlined in this book to help him control his impulsive behaviour. Although he still breaks out occasionally, he is doing well after two years of counselling.

If you do happen to fall in this category of impulsive gamblers, then in addition to reading this book, it is important for you to obtain additional counselling and support from a clinical psychologist in your community health service, and also to contact a psychiatrist or family doctor who can prescribe some anti-depressant medication or additional treatments that may be of help to you.

4

What is the effect of compulsive or problem gambling on the gambler?

Gambling to excess reduces a person's quality of life and his mental health. It also affects significant others: spouse or partner, parent or siblings. Mr A. B. is a 25-year-old married electrical technician who began gambling at the casino when he was eighteen. He attended the venue with several friends after a social event and won a reasonable amount of money from playing the roulette. This excited him and led him to believe that he had particular skills in picking winning numbers; he noticed that numbers in one of the sectors of the wheel were coming up more frequently. He then became a regular attendee at the casino, returning to his favourite table where he thought he could apply his logic in selecting numbers. He enjoyed discussing his strategy with his workmates and boasting of his skills.

Within twelve months he preferred to play by himself because this increased his opportunities to gamble over a longer time frame. He began to gamble almost daily, frequently taking time off work to do so. Losses did not worry him excessively because he could borrow money, go without or pawn possessions.

He married at age twenty-two. Although aware that he often went to the casino to play roulette, his wife did not realise the full extent of his gambling behaviour; and Mr A. B. was concerned that if she did, he would be forced to stop. Consequently, he concealed any evidence of his gambling. He also opened an Internet account with an overseas-regulated site so that he could play roulette without going to the casino. He did this to reduce complaints from his wife that he was coming home late from work or spending too much time away. To cover up his losses and keep his wife from discovering his Internet account, he opened secret bank and credit card accounts and started to juggle payments between the various accounts. This went on successfully for some time; however, eventually repeated losses meant that he had to take out loans. The debts mounted as he increased the size of each bet in the hope of winning enough to bail himself out.

His physical and emotional health started to deteriorate as a result of his constant preoccupation with his financial problems. He became moody and irritable and would often engineer arguments as an excuse to leave the house in order to place bets at the casino. These changes in his behaviour put stress on his relationship with his wife.

Soon he had exhausted all legitimate sources of borrowing and began to steal items from work to sell in order to obtain cash. In the meantime, his wife was becoming worried about the changes in his personality. Because of his absences from work and the increasing amount of time he was away from home, she came to the conclusion that he was having an affair.

Eventually his illegal activities were detected and the police called in to investigate. His wife was horrified, both by his being charged over the offences and the need to appear before the courts, and by the huge debt that he had incurred. There was a risk that the couple would have to sell the family home in order to repay it all and also cover their legal costs. Her trust in her husband was completely undermined and she was considering leaving him.

The case history of Peter, described briefly on pp.48–9, suggests several of the ways in which the pathological gambler will experience emotional distress as a result of his or her overall financial pressures caused by increasing losses. The effects impinge on emotions, behaviours, physical health and thought processes. Some examples of these effects will be discussed below.

Depression

I felt hopeless. Work no longer gave me any satisfaction. Nothing would perk me up, not even going to the cinema. Three thousand pounds in debt, I couldn't concentrate on meeting clients and selling the company products. I was wanting to read the form guide to select a winner in the next race, so I would cancel appointments or sell less just to get out of the meeting to listen to the race. My boss was on my back all the time and my wife needed a new washing machine. How was I to meet all these demands? Why can't people just leave me alone, I thought; all I want is to be left by myself. It got to the point where I no longer had the energy or the desire to put any effort into things. If only I could just lie in bed all day.

Clinical research has consistently revealed that up to 75 per cent of compulsive gamblers suffer from symptoms of major depression. The symptoms of depression are low mood, feeling 'blue', withdrawal from others, loss of appetite, no interest in activities, poor motivation, sleep disturbance and irritability. Physical symptoms often include headaches and a general sense of feeling poorly. For the depressed person the future seems to be very bleak indeed, as one cannot see any solution or escape out of the pit of unhappiness.

Some clinicians suggest that depression is one of the driving forces leading people to gamble compulsively in the first place, while others suggest that it is the logical consequence of deep financial and personal trouble. This issue is yet to be resolved. But what is clear is that mood disorders, substance abuse and stress reactions are a common feature found among problem gamblers. Unhappiness, loneliness and feeling poorly about yourself are hallmarks of the compulsive gambler; but they are hallmarks that can be removed.

Natalie gambled away her pension on the slot machines. She was five hundred pounds in debt on credit cards, was worried about her brother in a nursing home and upset over her daughter who was taking drugs. Living alone, she felt trapped in her situation, unable to see herself repaying her debts and being able to afford to live. For her, gambling was the only source of comfort and enjoyment in an otherwise empty life. Every night she would cry herself to sleep with worry.

In treatment, she was advised to seek assistance from a financial counsellor, who contacted her bank and arranged payments she could afford. Arrangements were also made for direct payments out of her pension to support her brother so that she did not have to worry or feel guilty that she was letting him down. Once help was being given to her daughter too, Natalie's mood started to improve and for the first time in a long while she began to look after her appearance, join in with other senior citizens on outings and feel better within herself. She says that she now cannot understand what she found in the slot machines and feels ill at any thought of going back to play them.

Suicidal thoughts

It is not surprising that many gamblers are highly distressed and panicky about their financial problems and the fear of being discovered by their spouse or partner, employer or the police if they have committed any offence or are in serious debt. The inability to see a solution, coupled with the low mood of depression, results in a sense of hopelessness, isolation and despair, while the deception and moodiness that go with pathological gambling put great strain on interpersonal relationships. This adds the fear that a partner or spouse will walk out, and anger and blame are directed toward oneself, weakening self-esteem. Alcohol abuse can exacerbate these feelings, which may eventually lead to suicidal ideas.

Let me illustrate the depth of the despair and poor judgment that can have tragic consequences for a few gamblers by citing from the transcript of a coroner's report into the death of a 32-year-old married man, found by his distraught wife hanging in the garage at his premises at about 11.50 a.m. on 20 September, 1995. His wife confirmed to the police that over the preceding nine months he had lost a considerable amount of money at the casino: thirteen thousand pounds in all, in three lots of two thousand, four thousand and seven thousand pounds. After each loss he promised he would never return. Arguments over finances were becoming increasingly common, and his wife had to take out a further loan of six thousand pounds to pay off a credit card.

On the night of 4 September, he withdrew five hundred pounds from the automatic teller machine at the casino. He was back the following night, stating to a friend that he wished to recoup his losses. During that night he lost one thousand pounds, and a friend described him as distressed. On 11 September he took the day off work and went to the casino, where he withdrew two hundred and fifty pounds. A similar pattern occurred on 15 September involving a larger amount of seven hundred and fifty pounds. All the monies were taken from his joint account, in which only seven pounds now remained. In a state of depression on the final evening, he consumed a large part of a 750 ml bottle of whisky and left a brief note stating that suicide was the only means by which he could escape his debts and marital problems. The coroner concluded: 'The deceased was known to be suffering from depression due to financial difficulties resulting from gambling at the casino, and the gradual breakdown of his marriage relationship.'

This is not an unusual case. Up to 60 per cent of compulsive gamblers think about suicide at some stage during a crisis, and around 20 per cent have taken steps to make actual suicide attempts. The true rate of suicide among problem gamblers is not known, because generally coroners and doctors attribute the cause of suicide to depression without recognising the crucial role that gambling may have played in causing the depression. As a result these deaths are not identified in the statistics of gambling-related suicides. Where statistics are held, it appears that in countries where gambling is widely available, about one suicide per month is recorded.

The risk of suicide is heightened if the person has a coexisting alcohol or drug problem or a family history of depression, or has committed serious criminal offences. In these circumstances, special attention should be given to offering as much support and encouragement as possible. Support from mental health professionals is strongly recommended in situations where suicidal thoughts or gestures have arisen. Blame and criticism do nothing more than aggravate the situation, so friends and family should be supportive.

Anxiety and anger

I explode at the drop of a hat. My kids avoid me; they're too scared to ask me to help with their homework because I yell at them. I just can't relax. Television just drives me batty, commercials and stupid shows. Yet I don't know what I want. I know I should be calmer and relate to my family but they don't understand. All they want is money for things, constant demands. I can't be expected to give them everything they want, can I? What about my needs? Don't I have a right to enjoy myself? What's wrong with a few bets?

It is not surprising that the stresses associated with compulsive gambling produce high states of anxiety and tension. These are expressed in feelings of agitation, excessive worry over the future, muscular tension and the inability to relax. Muscular tension is also often expressed in physical symptoms such as headaches, back pains and general feelings of fatigue and tiredness.

Sleep is disturbed because of the constant worry and agitation. The lack of sleep causes fatigue, compounding the irritability and poor tolerance of frustration. Many partners of gamblers complain that the gambler's mood fluctuates dramatically in response to trivial events or for no easily understood reason. In a small number of cases episodes of panic attacks may occur. These are brief periods of intense anxiety during which a person is convinced that he/she will die or lose sanity.

With tension and anxiety come short temper, irritability and outbursts of anger. There are reports that 15–20 per cent of compulsive gamblers express some anger toward family members and may even physically or verbally abuse their spouses or partners and children. Many of the people I have treated say that they deliberately engineer arguments in order to have an excuse to get out of the house to gamble. This also provides an opportunity for them to turn the argument around and place blame on the partner for causing tension, which 'forces' them to go off and gamble. 'If only she trusted me more, but she doesn't. If she thinks I'm gambling, damn it, I might as well do it, be hung for a sheep not a lamb' – these are words I often hear from clients. In a few instances, a man has hit his wife just to intimidate her so that she will think twice about questioning him over his behaviour and to get what he wants: money, time to gamble and silence. Many gamblers intimidate their spouses or partners to avoid social embarrassment by making sure that no one finds out about their gambling.

One of the main benefits offered by this self-help book is the relaxation technique it describes; while it is aimed primarily at controlling the gambling, it is reported by many gamblers to be helpful in calming their anxiety and anger in general. They say that, once they have grasped this technique, they no longer become easily angered but stay in control much more easily than before.

Alcohol consumption

I started to drink at first because it helped me to forget about the money I lost at the machines. I used to feel dreadful when I lost all my money. I thought, what will my wife say? I just didn't want to go home and face her.

Many people use alcohol and drugs to escape their worries and to overcome their feelings of anxiety or low self-confidence. It comes as no surprise to find that there is a high rate of coexisting alcohol- and drug-related problems in compulsive gamblers. Studies have shown that between 20 per cent and 40 per cent of such gamblers exhibit symptoms of alcoholism, while a smaller number, around 4–10 per cent, use illicit drugs. If you do drink excessively, then it is more likely that your gambling will be out of control and result in more severe problems. Remember, one of the effects of alcohol is to impair your judgment and make you feel overconfident in your own ability to win. You are more likely to take greater risks and to risk more money than you would otherwise.

Alcohol also affects self-control and interferes with your ability to avoid temptation or to stop gambling once started. Sometimes, excessive alcohol consumption causes a person to go on a single binge episode where a large amount of money is lost. The effect of this is devastating: the person starts to panic, drinks more in response to worry and then begins to borrow money to continue gambling to try to recoup losses. Recognising the signals and knowing how to respond under these circumstances is essential to minimise the harm. The section later in this book on how to stop chasing losses (Step 5 in Part Two) is particularly relevant here.

Alternatively, a person may lose excessive amounts of money during an individual gambling session, become depressed and then turn to alcohol to deaden the emotional and mental pain.

Those persons more at risk of developing alcohol and drug problems are those who have a family history of alcoholism, are suffering depression and anxiety, or exhibit signs of an anti-social personality, that is, a personality style characterised by disregard for social rules and conventions.

It is important to try to recognise within yourself what the main problem is. Is it the alcohol, the gambling or a combination of both? In other words, the question should be asked: is this a gambler who has an alcohol problem as a result of excessive gambling, or is this an alcoholic whose alcoholism leads him/her to lose control over gambling? This question must be addressed in order to gain a proper understanding of these disorders and an appropriate approach to their management. Attention must be given to teaching control over both forms of behaviour, otherwise one behaviour will act as a trigger for the other. The risk is that gambling will trigger an alcoholic to resume drinking because of the stress and depression associated with losing. Similarly, use of alcohol will trigger a gambling episode once the person is exposed to gambling cues.

One adolescent who was starting to do extremely well in treatment said that no one had picked up on the fact that he often spent time with his friends at the local bar. He would go with his friends and limit his drinking because he was the only one with a driver's licence. When his best friend obtained his licence, he felt that he could now drink more than his usual amount. On the second occasion, he felt confident in himself that he could control his gambling and thought that he should put himself to the test. He did well that time, so he thought he could continue – but promised himself that he would not go overboard. On the fourth occasion, he drank too much and began taking more risks. Predictably, he lost, felt that he had returned to square one and, in despair and anger at himself, gave up and started to binge in a self-destructive way. The whole process could have been halted if only he had learnt some of the simple strategies for relapse prevention outlined in this book.

Employment

I couldn't concentrate on work. Every half hour I would go to the toilet, sit down and be glued to my portable radio listening to the race broadcast. My boss finally suggested I see a doctor about my frequent need to use the toilet because he was worried about my health!

An exceedingly high proportion of gamblers report that their gambling has in some way interfered with their ability to perform effectively in their jobs. This interference with work takes the form of reduced productivity, absenteeism, poor concentration and attention, lost opportunities for promotion, failure to follow up potential sales or new clients, and not showing initiative. Also, constant attempts to borrow from colleagues and failure to repay debts, and the desire to conceal the level of gambling, can lead to social isolation from colleagues.

In about 30 per cent of cases the problems associated with gambling have led to resignation or termination of employment. Resignation is a step taken by many to avoid being detected or prosecuted for misappropriation, embezzlement or theft from petty cash. One gambler employed as a car parts salesman reported persistently stealing and selling spare parts to acquaintances to finance his gambling. This occurred in all three jobs he held in that industry and again in another non-related industry before he was caught and charged. His pattern was to leave each job as soon as he believed his supervisors suspected that he was the culprit.

What is of especial interest is the amount of time and effort some people are prepared to put into gambling and losing money, while avoiding placing a similar amount of effort into their work, which should be personally and financially more rewarding. Some gamblers show exceptional talents that, if directed to their work, would result in personal satisfaction and significant business success. Stephen was an accountant of outstanding abilities who, over a period of two years, embezzled one hundred thousand pounds from his computer company. Only a small fraction of his fraud was detected, and that only by accident. It was only when he cooperated with the police and his auditors that the true extent and ingenuity of his crime were discovered. He then proceeded to instruct his employers on how to strengthen the security of their accounting system to prevent future fraud. The company was impressed with his knowledge and hard work and offered him a job on his release from prison – but of course with restricted access to cash, 'just to be safe and for peace of mind,' said the general manager.

Lying and deceit

Lying is a way of life now. It's easier to tell my husband I've been visiting Jill and a few of the mothers from pre-school than telling him that I spent several hours playing bingo.

The further the gambler moves toward the desperation phase of gambling, the greater is the pressure to conceal their behaviour, so that lying becomes an automatic part of everyday living. Lies become more frequent as the gambler attempts to explain: unaccounted time away from the family or work, lack of money to pay bills, mood swings and phone calls from creditors.

Additional pressure is placed on the gambler after domestic arguments and promises never to gamble again. The following cycle is so commonly described that it almost appears to be a universal truth. First comes the promise to change. This is followed by a short period of improvement, then by more gambling. Once a gambling episode has occurred, there is pressure to keep losses hidden and to gamble more to win back the money before the loss is detected. The gambler cannot afford to disclose the lapse to his/her spouse or partner because of the promise already made. Then comes discovery: the cover has been blown. Arguments ensue; the gambler expresses remorse and promises never to gamble again – with an assurance that this time it is really genuine. And so the cycle begins again.

What is important is that gamblers trapped in this repeated cycle have not yet learnt the necessary skills and strategies that will assist them in identifying the steps leading to a relapse and taking alternative positive action that will immediately reduce their motivation to resume gambling. I have found that the person who responds well to therapy is the one who tells his or her spouse or partner openly of an urge to gamble as soon as it is felt. The very act of admitting the impulse to one's spouse or partner is often sufficient to abort the urge. Another benefit of open and honest communication is that one's partner is kept informed of what is happening and therefore soon begins to regain trust. It is the uncertainty of knowing whether or not one's spouse is gambling and what debts are being accumulated that is so stressful and distressing.

Cognitive impairment

'Cognitive functioning' is a term used to refer to one's intellectual activity, which includes thinking, memory, problem-solving, concentration and reasoning. It is only to be expected that stresses resulting from the conflict over the simultaneous urge to gamble and awareness of the need to stop, plus persistent worries over the problems being caused by gambling and the fear of being found out, will lead to problems in these areas. There is interference in one's ability to think clearly, make decisions with confidence and retain new information. Forgetfulness is common; in some cases, concentration and attention are so poor that the person has difficulty reading and understanding newspapers or following the plot of a television show. These symptoms are related to stress and with proper management can be quickly reversed.

Physical symptoms

The pathological gambler's physical health deteriorates rapidly under conditions of chronic stress: juggling disappearing finances, hiding evidence of all gambling activity and debts, chasing losses and attempting to maintain some semblance of normality to others. Headaches, high blood pressure, anxiety symptoms, fatigue and poor sleep are symptoms commonly reported. People just feel down, washed out and physically exhausted, with general complaints of aches and pains.

We know that constant worry and anxiety can eventually lead to stress-related physical symptoms. Symptoms of this kind, resulting from an underlying psychological stress, constitute what is called psychosomatic illness. The most commonly reported symptoms are:

- headaches;
- high blood pressure;
- gastro-intestinal problems such as nervous diarrhoea;
- general muscular aches and pains;
- disturbed sleep and excessive fatigue;
- other specific problems such as skin rashes.

Tackling the underlying stress by, for example, using the relaxation and other techniques described in Part Two of this book, can rapidly alleviate these distressing physical conditions.

5

What is the impact of compulsive or problem gambling on family members and others?

The impact of gambling on the welfare of the gambler's partner and family can be extensive. The consequent financial difficulties in particular cause strain and friction within the family. Often the partner experiences a sense of betrayal, anger or despair and may suffer stress-related disorders. In a study of the spouses of gamblers, Valerie Lorenz, an American therapist, found that many reported suffering multiple psychosomatic symptoms including headaches, gastrointestinal disturbances, poor sleep and general malaise, and frequently consulted their family doctor. Sexual relationships, too, deteriorated as a result of a lack of communication, pervasive tension, unexpressed feelings of anger and low self-esteem.

What is most disappointing for many spouses or partners is that apart from the gambling behaviour, they love their partners and see them as wonderful and caring people. If only the gambling stopped, they say, their relationship would be ideal. Perhaps this explains why many partners stay with and support their partners despite their repeated broken promises and continued gambling. But while the gambling goes on, domestic arguments frequently occur. Conflicts arise as a result of the stress caused by continual financial difficulties and by the accompanying frequent lies to conceal the level of gambling going on.

Partners also experience frustration and a sense of failure in not being able to persuade their other half to seek treatment. Pleas to make an appointment with a counsellor fall on deaf ears and often lead to further arguments. Information on gambling treatment services and counselling left in plain view around the house for the gambling partner to read are either ignored or thrown out. This sense of inability on the part of the spouse, boyfriend or girlfriend to help their gambling partner is profound and results in both emotional and physical stress affecting their overall wellbeing. Under these circumstances, partners ought to consider seeking assistance from counsellors to deal with this sense of helplessness.

Children in such living circumstances suffer considerably when exposed to a climate of tension, arguments and hostility, leading them to display signs of disturbed conduct and behaviour. The effects of gambling on children are poorly researched, but we have a good understanding of the child's reaction to family arguments and to parental separation in general: the child responds with confusion, depression and a sense of low self-worth. The gambler is often absent but, when present, is irritable, edgy and withdrawn. Constant arguments between parents create an environment of tension and fear. Tragically, some studies have shown that possibly a fifth of problem gamblers perpetrate acts of child physical abuse or domestic violence against their partners.

In summary, marital friction is shown in:

- frequent arguments between couples;
- the gambler's withdrawal from family outings and interactions;
- lack of funds for family activities;
- abusive behaviour by the gambler;
- periods of marital separation;
- divorce.

It is clear that excessive gambling will eventually result in the build-up of debts that cannot be met. The lack of available money to meet the basic costs of daily living expenses and fixed repayments results in the family not being able to:

- pay for emergency/unexpected repairs to house or car;
- meet rent/mortgage payments and utility bills;
- afford family holidays;
- afford social or leisure activities for family members;
- purchase gifts for special occasions;
- have enough disposable income for occasional extra needs.

The constant financial pressure increases the stress on the gambler, who becomes ever more worried and preoccupied as a result, and consequently ever more detached from the family and particularly sensitive to any questions that may be raised regarding the household's financial condition. Outbursts of irritability and anger become commonplace.

Eventually access to money is limited, forcing the gambler to seek other sources of funds. These include:

- spending savings (own or spouse's);
- cashing assets such as pension funds, shares or bonds;
- cashing in holiday and/or sick-pay allowances;
- drawing cash advances from credit-card accounts;
- taking out high-interest loans;
- pawning jewellery and electrical goods;
- accessing bank accounts of family members without their knowledge;
- engaging in criminal activities such as embezzlement, theft or burglary.

In the vast majority of cases, the spouse is unaware of what is happening and of the level of financial debt.

To avoid detection the gambler begins to be deceitful and dishonest, resorting to frequent lies and excuses to explain why bills are not paid or purchases/holidays cannot be afforded.

The following are some of the many stratagems used by gamblers to conceal problems from their families:

- inventing excuses as to why they cannot afford purchases;
- redirecting bills to post office boxes so that the spouse/partner remains unaware of unpaid or overdue bills;
- intercepting the mail before the spouse/partner has a chance to see what is coming in to the household;
- refusing to allow the spouse/partner to open mail;
- picking up bank statements directly from the bank;
- forging the spouse/partner's signature on loan applications or other documents;
- pawning items of value and then claiming these to be lost or stolen.

These stratagems may be successfully applied for several years, with partners, family members and relatives remaining oblivious to their deteriorating financial circumstances. At times a partner may be perplexed and worried over the gambler's behaviour; often, too, lack of interest in him- or herself or in the family, a preoccupied manner, lack of money and time spent away from home may lead a partner to assume that the gambler is having an affair or has a problem with alcoholism.

Discovery of the true situation often comes alarmingly suddenly and from unexpected sources:

- bank statements revealing large loans or overdue bills;
- deposit account statements revealing the loss of savings and assets;
- credit-card statements showing frequent and large cash advances;
- pawn tickets for items claimed to have been lost or stolen;
- forged signatures on documents;
- police visiting to interview the gambler or to level charges for offences committed;
- receipt of legal notices threatening repossession or similar action.

A spouse/partner's reactions to the discovery of gambling debts

Spouses and partners go through a series of complex and confusing emotions as they become aware of what is happening behind their backs. Their dreams, expectations and future plans are shattered as they realise that they are no longer in a financially secure position. What is most damaging and challenging is confronting the reality that the person to whom they are married and on whom they thought they could depend has been repeatedly deceitful and playing them for a fool. Trust of any type has evaporated.

A spouse/partner may experience a mixture of distressing emotions or may go through a process in which a series of feelings emerge over time. There is no consistent pattern, but the predominant sequence is as follows:

Confusion

- Stunned disbelief of what has happened.
- Questioning if it is really happening or whether some unfortunate mistake has occurred.
- Self-doubt: 'Is it my fault? Did I cause him/her to gamble?'

Guilt

- 'I should have picked up the signals earlier.'
- 'If only I had realised then I could have prevented this situation.'

- 'It was my behaviour or our relationship that caused him/her to gamble, I did not give him/her enough attention.'

Anger

- 'How could he/she do this to our family?'
- 'I have worked hard to save or to enable him/her to save for a new house or holiday and now he/she has lost it all.'
- 'How could he/she be so selfish as to spend our hard-earned money on himself/herself in such a useless activity?'

Loss of trust

- 'I can no longer trust him/her.'
- 'What else has he/she done behind my back?'
- 'How can I ever believe what he/she tells me?'

Worry for the future

- 'What does this mean for the future?'
- 'How can we get ourselves out of this situation?'
- 'How will I get a job to help keep our heads above water?'
- 'Is he/she going to gamble again and cause further problems?'

The most worrying aspect is the loss of trust – the very foundation of any marital relationship. With lack of trust comes uncertainty: uncertainty as to whether you know the whole picture or whether there are other similar problems remaining that the gambler has yet to reveal. This uncertainty is reinforced when newer debts or problems are revealed. Most spouses or partners don't know the full extent of the problems generated by their partners' excessive gambling, and they live in constant fear and suspense that another major crisis will reveal itself shortly.

The other major uncertainty is the question of continued gambling. Having deceived the spouse/partner in the past, will the gambler again at some future point recommence gambling and plunge the household into another downward spiral of financial woes?

With the lack of trust and uncertainty come strong feelings of insecurity and fear.

The typical response of the gambler to discovery is to

deny or minimise the situation by arguing that the situation is not as bad as it appears, that they have a plan of action that will get them out of their problems or that this is a 'one-off' aberration that they will never repeat. Many gamblers show remorse and contrition, promising fervently that they will never repeat their mistake or gamble again.

If the spouse/partner reacts with anger, the gambler may defend him- or herself by manipulating emotions. She/he may attempt to transfer guilt and blame to the partner by arguing that it was his/her fault that she/he gambled in the first place. He/she may act as the victim and attempt to draw sympathy and concern from the partner or spouse. Alternatively, he/she may act helpless and dependent, eliciting emotions of sympathy and sorrow for his/her plight. By so doing, the cause of the problem is again shifted from the gambler to his/her partner, who is now seen as being responsible for the excessive gambling and therefore responsible for solving the problem.

This book may assist a gambler's spouse, partner, close friend or employer to understand the nature of gambling. Partners may also need assistance and guidance in learning how to deal with the stresses of their situation and advice on how to respond to demands placed on them. It is advisable for them to seek help from Gam-Anon, a self-help organisation aimed at helping the partners of pathological gamblers, or treatment from qualified clinical psychologists, psychiatrists or other health professionals such as general practitioners or social workers familiar with the problems of pathological gambling. Referral to these specialists may be sought from local community health service facilities. Gam-Anon meetings are held at the same time as the Gamblers Anonymous meetings for the gambler. Details of meetings can be obtained from the Gamblers Anonymous contact number listed in your local telephone directory or through a search on the Internet.

It is strongly recommended that assistance from health services is sought for two reasons: firstly, to manage and maintain their own mental health and a sense of stability and control, and, secondly, to receive advice on ways and means to encourage and motivate the gambling partner to seek assistance.

Gamblers, crime and the law

In one of the saddest cases I have come across, Morris, a 59-year-old librarian, was addicted to slot machine gambling for ten years. He resorted to any means possible to obtain money. Once he paid a woman he met on the street to pretend to be his wife while he extended a loan from an account jointly held with his wife. What really undermined his self-esteem and caused his depression to plummet was another episode in a club where, as he walked past a woman sitting at a table, he quickly kicked her handbag away, picked it up and took it to the toilet where, quivering with anticipation, he rummaged through the purse and removed all the money. The bag also contained a passport and other important documents, but at the time the anxiety and inconvenience he was creating for the bag's owner was of little concern to him: he thought no further than satisfying his own needs. Only later, in the calm of the aftermath, did the full impact of his action bring him down emotionally. Even so, several days later he shamefully confessed that he was out looking for a similar opportunity when he needed money again. Guilt dissolved in the face of gratifying his needs.

Morris is not an isolated instance. Research has revealed that 60 per cent of pathological gamblers commit some criminal offence in order to support their gambling habits. The gravity of these offences ranges from theft from their partner's bank account or writing cheques knowing that there are insufficient funds in the account, through taking money from petty cash to serious and premeditated fraud and embezzlement. It is sobering to note that 22 per cent of pathological gamblers have been charged for offences, and 12–15 per cent have been convicted of such offences.

Gamblers commit criminal offences when legal sources of funds are totally exhausted and to enable them to:

- continue the gambling habit;
- attempt to recoup losses;
- repay money borrowed from friends;
- meet repayments to financial institutions for loans taken out;
- obtain money to repay debts and cover shortfalls incurred because of gambling;
- cover up losses and avoid detection by partner, employer or friends.

Typically, it is found that the gambler commits about ten offences involving amounts of one hundred and fifty pounds each. However, it is worth noting that 15–20 per cent engage in offences relating to amounts of ten thousand pounds or more. I have known of or personally treated at least ten gamblers who have appeared in court for offences involving sums exceeding one million pounds.

What is tragic is that the majority of gamblers who offend show no evidence of any other criminal behaviour and do not have a past history of anti-social behaviour or conflict with the law. It is clear from research data that most gamblers are led into crime as a result of their excessive gambling and the need to cover it up. This, of course, enables them to argue that they are not fully responsible for their own behaviour; and yet gamblers *do* know what they are doing and *are* aware that what they are doing is wrong. Consequently, they cannot argue that they should have consideration at law on account of a condition called 'pathological gambling' or a 'gambling disorder'.

Some gamblers fall foul of the law when they forget, or are unaware, that some behaviour may be regarded by some people as acceptable when it is technically illegal. We have had two or three cases where a person was in serious trouble for failing to bank income from sales on the Friday, using the money to gamble over the weekend and then replacing the funds later the following week. Their employers laid charges against them for unauthorised use of company money. The rule is simple: if it is not yours, then do not spend it; and gambling is spending.

Social problems

Gambling has a major impact on social and family life, affecting not only the gambler but, most importantly, the spouse or partner and children, not to mention other relatives including parents. The preoccupation with gambling, fear that others may discover the true extent of one's behaviour and financial predicament all motivate the gambler to shun social contact. Social occasions that conflict with gambling opportunities are avoided. Excuses are made not to attend or, if attending, to leave at odd times so that bets may be placed. Family outings, especially on Saturdays, no longer happen. No efforts are made to go out to restaurants, shows or indeed any activities that cost money that otherwise could be gambled. The preoccupation with gambling virtually eliminates any enjoyment of or motivation to participate in non-gambling-related leisure pursuits. Repeated refusals of invitations to go out with friends lead to such invitations becoming fewer and less frequent. Marital arguments over financial matters and gambling make it unpleasant for the couple to be together in public, and to avoid embarrassment it is much easier to remain at home. Others feel uncomfortable to be around a couple who are always arguing.

Because of the social embarrassment of not having enough money to buy clothes and goods, the partner of a gambler may not wish to talk to friends, and may instead avoid any situation where such subjects are raised and where it might be necessary to lie in order to cover up the true situation.

The social impact on the family is aggravated by the gambler's behaviour resulting in him/her:

- becoming socially withdrawn and isolated;
- losing friends;
- becoming less motivated to engage in any activities other than gambling;
- becoming irritable, tense and moody when pressured by family members to attend social functions that interfere with gambling.

The overall picture of the gambler and his or her family is an unhappy one. But, as we shall see in the next chapter and in Part Two of this book, it is possible successfully to treat problem gambling, to the great and lasting benefit not only of gamblers but of those around them too.

6

How can problem gambling be treated?

Effective treatment of problem gambling is available. There are many clinical studies that have shown a range of treatment interventions that lead to successful outcomes. It is stressed that compulsive gambling *is* treatable and that many people are able to improve their quality of life as a result of undertaking treatment. No matter how desperate the situation may seem at the time, by taking the proper steps outlined in Part Two of this book, control over behaviour can be regained.

Psychological treatments

Several psychological treatments have been used to help people with gambling problems. Between 1914 and 1957 the only approach offered by mental health professionals was psychoanalytic or psychodynamic in orientation. It was argued that gamblers had an unconscious drive to punish themselves as a result of unresolved Oedipal complexes. The few case studies reported in the literature were not systematically evaluated over reasonable follow-up periods.

Two important events in the late 1950s and early 1960s, one in the USA and the other in the UK, had an important influence in shaping the direction of gambling treatment. First, Gamblers Anonymous was established in 1957. This is a self-help group based on the same philosophy and approach as Alcoholics Anonymous. This organisation worked closely with the late Dr Robert Custer, a psychiatrist who established the first hospital gambling programme at the Veterans' Administration in Brecksville, Ohio in 1972. Through Dr Custer's efforts, compulsive or pathological gambling came to be recognised as a psychiatric disorder in 1980 following its inclusion in the American Psychiatric Association's *Diagnostic and Statistical Manual of Mental Disorders*. Earlier, in 1975, pathological gambling was included in the International Classification of Diseases as a behavioural disorder but did not gain much traction until later.

Because of the close association between Gamblers Anonymous and Custer's programme, compulsive gambling in America quickly came to be regarded as an addiction. Earlier, programmes to treat it were offered in drug and alcohol facilities and often placed a heavy emphasis on attendance at Gamblers Anonymous meetings. Programmes have expanded and are now being offered in a variety of gambling specialist counselling and community and hospital health service facilities; these include government-funded and non-government agencies.

The second event was a sad case of brain surgery carried out in the UK in 1973. A 21-year-old Cheshire ice-cream seller was convicted of stealing to support a gambling habit. The magistrate, with the agreement of the patient and his mother, referred the matter to a neurosurgeon, who performed psychosurgery on the man. No records remain of the case but this radical form of intervention caused an uproar within the mental health field. This controversy prompted several British psychologists and psychiatrists to turn to behavioural treatments, in particular aversion therapy. In this form of therapy, mild electric shocks were given to the fingers while a person played the slot machines or watched a horse race. Shocks were administered randomly during various stages of slot-machine play, reading racing form guides, watching audio-visually presented gambling stimuli or reading gambling-related phrases written on cards. The shocks delivered to the fingers were of an unpleasant but not painful nature. The idea was to form a new association between an activity that was previously pleasurable and an aversive or unpleasant stimulus. While effective with about up to a quarter of gamblers, the technique involved causing the gambler some discomfort and was not very popular with many therapists.

More recently, motivational interviewing and cognitive behavioural therapies coupled with relapse-prevention techniques are proving to be a highly effective alternative treatment route. Part Two of this book concentrates on cognitive behavioural techniques in the management of problem gambling. The rest of this chapter outlines the cognitive behavioural approach to therapy and describes briefly the role that can be played by medication, particularly in light of recent psychopharmacological advances in drug therapy. Additional detailed information on the foundation of cognitive behaviour therapy as applied to pathological gambling can be found in Michael Walker's comprehensive book, *The Psychology of Gambling* (see the 'Useful reading' section at the end of this book). But before we embark on this explanation, a brief word about motivational interviewing.

Motivational interviewing accepts that many people are ambivalent about changing behaviours, particularly those that provide some reward, relief or psychological benefits, even those behaviours that may also prove to result in some discomfort or pain. Examples are overeating, alcohol and drug dependence and, of course, gambling. Counselling strategies that are confrontational in style are not highly effective in achieving desired outcomes. In contrast, those that are empathic, non-judgmental and supportive in approach are more likely to sway an individual into committing to change. Accordingly, motivational interviewing is based on the premise that individuals expressing a strong personal commitment to change behaviours, that is, a readiness to change, will be more likely to achieve their goals.

Readiness to change is fostered by having an individual evaluate the benefits and costs of ceasing gambling in a non-judgmental and supportive atmosphere. How is this managed? Firstly, by pointing out that being uncertain about wanting to change is normal, and that the motivation to change also fluctuates over time. The aim is to have an individual compare the type of person he or she has become as a result of the gambling with the type of person he or she would like to be, and how he or she would like others to see him or her. The focus is on drawing attention to the individual's strengths and ability to achieve change. This is done by helping him or her to identify and correct faulty beliefs and ways of thinking. Finally, pointing out the benefits of changing rather than continuing their self-destructive path will increase motivations to change.

Motivational interviewing has been shown to be effective with comparable outcomes to cognitive behavioural interventions obtained. Once an individual is committed to change and shares the same goals as the therapist, the chance of a successful outcome is increased dramatically. The next step is to find out how a gambler thinks.

How do gamblers think?

'Cognitions' are mental activities such as thoughts, beliefs, attitudes, images and memories, which together form a person's schema or mental representation of the self, others and the world in general. A schema contains an organised set of core beliefs about specific things. For example, a gambler may view him- or herself as someone who has fewer skills and abilities than others but has high expectations to succeed placed on them by parents. Statements may include: 'I must please my parents otherwise they will reject me as a worthless person'; 'To be accepted I must provide my children with whatever they want – a new computer, holidays, etc.'; 'Gambling is one way of getting money quickly so I can impress my wife by giving her what she wants.'

It is by identifying and correcting distorted or irrational ways of thinking that a person can start to take proper steps to overcome gambling. For example, a typical statement given by many gamblers in debt is: 'I owe so much I will never pay it off by working. The only way I can get enough money is by winning at the races.' They forget that gambling created the debt in the first place. If gambling led you to debt, then how will more gambling eliminate your debt? Surely, the end result of more gambling can only be an increase in how much you owe?

Here is another good example of how differently from non-gamblers gamblers think. The odds of winning a lottery may be two million to one. A non-gambler would say to him- or herself, 'The odds are against me, I am unlikely to win so I won't buy a ticket.' A gambler would say, 'Hey, someone has to win, that someone could be me. You've got to be in it to win it. I've been close several times; it must be my turn to win soon.' Advertisements promoting gambling emphasise this point by suggesting that everyone can be a winner, and exhorting you not to miss your turn.

What is cognitive therapy?

Making decisions is a complex task that is influenced by many factors. This is particularly true under conditions of uncertainty. Two processes in decision-making are relevant for our purposes here. The first is what is called heuristic thinking. Decisions are made quickly and almost automatically on the basis of past experiences and previous learning.

Many factors are simultaneously taken into account without giving too much thought; it results in decisions that are interpreted as 'intuition' or 'acting on a hunch'. In contrast, the second process relies more on a linear logical sequence of thinking through to the final decision. Each option or element is carefully considered and evaluated before deciding what action will be taken. Cognitive theory takes into account decision-making processes and errors of thinking associated with these.

Although there are a number of different cognitive models, the common thread shared by all is that cognitions directly influence your behaviour, that automatic thoughts (heuristic thinking) can be brought to conscious awareness and monitored, that irrational cognitions can be altered and that altering such cognition leads to changes in one's behaviour. What is an automatic thought? It is fascinating to note that many people are not consciously aware of the thought processes that operate to influence behaviour. An automatic thought is literally a habit, a thought that occurs so often and so fast that you no longer become aware of its existence. Let me illustrate with an example. How many times have you driven a car and, while driving, become so engrossed in your own thoughts that you drive several miles without really concentrating on what you were doing? This is a normal phenomenon. You were able to change gears, watch out for traffic and safely control the car. Yet you were not consciously aware of your actions while driving. You were relying on automatic reactions that allowed you to do one thing while being mentally preoccupied with something else.

The same applies in gambling. Decisions are made that lead one to 'suddenly' finding oneself in a gambling setting. One does not remember how one came to be there. This is an example of automatic thinking.

In principle, therefore, the aim of cognitive therapy is to assist the gamblers in setting about systematically identifying distorted or irrational thoughts, challenging these faulty assumptions and replacing them with correct styles of thinking.

Distorted thinking in problem gamblers

Let us briefly look at some of the more common faulty thoughts and ways of thinking that lead people to continue gambling despite the obvious problems it creates. The steps showing how one may correct these will be provided in more detail in Part Two of this book.

Most gamblers like to believe that they have some skill or ability to influence the outcome of a chance event. The roulette player will study the pattern of numbers and place bets accordingly, the slot-machine player believes that pressing the button with a certain pressure will influence the spin and lottery players will have their favourite winning numbers. The sports bettor will believe that they can predict the better team on the day based on the knowledge they have of each player, the team or sport. There is some research evidence to support the notion of what E. J. Langer has called the 'illusion of control' – the belief that a gambler can alter the outcome of a chance event. It is related quite closely to superstitious behaviour, that is, carrying a lucky charm that the gambler believes gives him or her an additional edge to influence the outcome.

Illusions of control are strengthened by a process of what the American psychologist Thomas Gilovich calls 'biased evaluation'. Simply put, this means that people will remember and recall wins more than losses, and will further attribute wins to their own skill or ability. Losses are easily forgotten, pushed out of mind or explained away as the fault of some other unforeseen influence. How many times have you heard the statement, 'The horse would have won had it not stumbled at the starting gate,' or 'The jockey was obviously holding him back'? However, when a long shot comes in, one always accepts that it is because of skill and good judgment, not pure luck or a fluke: 'I knew it would win, that's why I bet on it at such long odds.' The win serves to strengthen belief in one's own level of skill.

Many gamblers profess a solid knowledge of the mathematics of chance, but their behaviour does not reflect it. Playing roulette, a gambler will not bet on a number that has just come up because they believe it has a lower probability of coming up twice in a row. Similarly, in tossing a coin, if five heads in a row are tossed, most people will argue that the next toss will have a higher probability of coming up tails. This is incorrect. The next toss will have a one in two chance of a head or tail irrespective of how many heads came before it. The toss of a coin is not dependent on what came up in the toss before; any two tosses are mutually independent events.

In picking lottery numbers, say a series of six out of forty, most people will pick evenly spread numbers, for example, 1, 9, 15, 21, 34, 39. They believe that a series such as 1, 2, 3, 4, 5, 6 has a very much lower chance of coming up than one that is more evenly spread. This is wrong. Both series have as much chance as each other of coming up. Indeed, numbers picked at random do not show a consistent pattern of being evenly spread out but tend to cluster together; for example, all six numbers may be under 20, or there may be a sequence of two or three consecutive numbers such as 12, 13, 14. Try it and see.

Some gamblers will personify a favourite machine. By this I mean that they will start to talk to it as though it were a real being with whom they are interacting: 'Come on, baby, this time you've got to give it to me'; 'What's wrong, have I upset you?'; or 'Damn you, let me win or I won't ever play you again.'

Some gamblers believe that they can win at gambling. These gamblers will usually relate a story of how they won a large amount of money. This proves that they can win, they say. But when you ask them what they did with the winnings, most say they re-gambled it, or bought something that they then had to pawn to get more money to gamble. What they need to do is to increase the time frame they are considering. For example, if a person enters a session with one hundred pounds, wins a million pounds, continues gambling and at the end of the session leaves with fifty pounds in his pocket, how much has he won (or lost)? The hard-core gambler would say he won a million pounds, the realist would say he lost fifty pounds. How you interpret these wins or losses will strongly influence the extent to which you feel frustrated and angry and the degree to which you want to continue gambling.

It is important to realise that distorted cognition may play a part at any stage of the gambling cycle. It may lead you to believe that you have a much greater level of skill or control in influencing outcomes than you really have. It may lead you to filter out losses you had and to recall instead only the wins, giving you a wrong impression of having won more than you lost. It may influence the strength of your belief that you are about to win because of the number of close calls you've had. Machine manufacturers use this tendency to manipulate your behaviour. Every so often a near-winning combination appears, giving rise to the expectation that the jackpot is due very soon. Nothing is further from the truth. This is a carrot to keep you involved and playing. Such 'near wins' also lead the gambler to think that a losing streak is about to end.

Additional cognitive distortions can be found where the gambler has an over-optimistic belief in her own luck, for example, that things always turn out in her favour eventually. These people may be superstitious. How many times have you repeated a pattern of doing something, worn some favourite piece of clothing or item, sat at the same seat at bingo or always played your 'own' favourite machine? Some people will carry lucky charms or a lucky coin, or go through a ritual of touching a part of the machine to guarantee themselves good luck. While realising that such behaviour is superstitious and does not really influence outcome, people still hold these beliefs and practise these habits 'just in case; after all it doesn't do any harm.'

A few people, perhaps more than we imagine, hold a strong belief that they somehow have a greater level of inbuilt special skills, knowledge or other natural talents that give them a winning 'edge' over other gamblers. This applies more to people who gamble frequently. Their level of skill varies but it has been shown that many, in particular the younger gamblers, make reference to knowledge or familiarity with reel positions on fruit machines and the manual operations of buttons. They believe that they have better skills and a better chance of winning than others. The same applies with card games and knowledge of statistics and skills of bluffing, and sports betting, where one believes that one can estimate which team will win based on knowing players and their skill levels. It is interesting to see that belief in one's skill and ability to win persists despite the obvious evidence of continued losses. This is because people dismiss losses by attributing them to other factors: for example, someone else played the machine and broke the sequence, or the team lost because of poor refereeing.

Correcting one's core beliefs about gambling and about the chances of winning are crucial to overcoming uncontrolled gambling. However, there are a number of other factors that need to be taken into account and modified. One needs to be taught how to control the urge to gamble once it arises. Use of relaxation-based techniques, as described in

Part Two of this book, is fundamental to success. Where depression occurs, one must take steps to reduce the low mood in order to increase motivation, the chances of compliance with treatment instructions and the hope that gambling and gambling problems can be overcome and solved. Use of medication under your family doctor's or psychiatrist's direction may be beneficial. Strategies to avoid exposure to gambling triggers may need to be applied. For those who suffer from an additional problem of alcohol or drug dependence, it is imperative that some help is directed to overcoming this problem, because it will determine how successful your efforts will be to regain control over gambling. All of these factors need to be addressed. By following each and every step in this book, as well as possibly consulting other relevant books in this series and seeking help from your family doctor or community health centre, you will have set yourself on the pathway to recovery.

Medications

A limited range of medications are used in the treatment of pathological gambling. These drugs are helpful because of their indirect effect on improving mood or reducing impulsivity, but very little useful information about their effectiveness is available. Remember, there is no drug that eliminates the urge to gamble or impulsivity altogether. Medication therapy should not be used alone but in conjunction with other, psychological approaches, such as the cognitive behavioural approach described in this book.

Some studies have found lithium carbonate to be mildly beneficial in moderating mood fluctuations that appear linked to gambling behaviour, particularly where a diagnosis of bipolar illness is found. Some people suffering mania or hypomanic episodes experience elevated mood, exaggerated feelings of confidence and impaired judgment, which may result in prolonged episodes of excessive gambling. To illustrate, one police constable would periodically engage in severe bouts of gambling when he was in a high mood. He spent a whole week gambling virtually non-stop, amassing debts of several thousand pounds but confident in the belief that he would become a millionaire. He took out substantial loans and pawned jewellery. These cases are usually easy to identify because of the bizarre or unusual pattern of behaviour, and the fact that their intensity of gambling behaviours are closely related to elevated mood states.

The main use of medication, however, is to control depression. Anti-depressant drugs, such as the tricyclics (e.g. imipramine, amitriptyline) or monoamine oxidase inhibitors (e.g. phenelzine), are useful where the depression is so severe that it represents a risk of suicide. In other circumstances the gambler may be so depressed that any motivation to comply with therapeutic instructions is lost, or the future is seen as so bleak that any effort to resolve problems seems futile. If you suffer from depression, it is important to consult your family doctor for advice on whether an antidepressant medication may be of benefit.

Selective serotonin reuptake inhibitors (SSRIs) merit special mention. A number of biological studies have indicated possible evidence for disturbances in the regulation of certain classes of brain neurotransmitters (serotonin, dopamine and norepinephrine or noradrenaline). These naturally occurring brain substances regulate arousal, mood, impulsivity and responses to reward and punishment. Studies from my clinic have shown that gamblers obtain high scores on psychological measures of impulsivity, that is, making quick decisions without worrying about their consequences. There appears to be a positive association between impulsivity and level of gambling: that is, the higher the score on psychological measures of impulsivity, the greater is the severity of the disturbance caused by excessive gambling. Also, a high proportion of gamblers suffer significant depression, and it has also been proposed that some people use gambling as a means of overcoming their depression. Although there are a few reports in the literature suggesting that the SSRI medications are effective, it remains unclear whether they work by reducing the depression or by their action in dampening impulsivity.

Dr Eric Hollander has noted the similarities between impulse control disorders, including gambling, and other repetitive behaviours, including eating disorders and obsessive-compulsive neurosis. He and his colleagues argue that pathological gambling lies along part of an obsessive-compulsive spectrum of disorders. As a result of this hypothesis, medications used to treat obsessional disorders (e.g. clomipramine and SSRIs) have been used to treat gamblers.

There is another class of drugs that has been used to decrease gambling urges. These fall within the class referred to as opioid antagonists such as Naltrexone. We know that opioids are naturally occurring brain chemicals that are associated with 'highs' and positive mood states, and that Naltrexone is a drug that blocks these effects. We all know of the 'jogger's high' and the highs associated with certain classes of drugs and alcohol. Blocking these naturally occurring opioids acts to prevent the 'high' response experienced after consuming a substance or acting out certain behaviours. The more frequently one consumes or acts but does not experience the 'high', the more the urge to consume or act reduces. This is known as extinction: that is, with repeated use that is not reinforced, the less the person will be motivated to consume or act. Naltrexone, an opioid antagonist, is often used in treating heroin abuse based on this principle; the less the high experienced, the lower the motivation to continue.

Do consult your psychiatrist or family doctor; they will guide you as to the most suitable medication for your individual needs. Remain aware that the evidence supporting the effectiveness of many of the medications used to manage gambling remains mixed.

The goals of treatment: Abstinence or control?

A large percentage of gamblers are in conflict when it comes to goals of treatment, torn between a strong desire to continue and an equally strong aversion to the concept of completely giving up gambling. Why is this?

The gambler's dilemma

There are several reasons for this ambivalence. As we have already noted, gambling is an intrinsically exciting and physically arousing behaviour. Laboratory studies have shown rapid increases in heart rate of up to fifty beats per minute under gambling conditions. Even when the return to a player is less than the stake wagered, individuals respond in almost strikingly similar ways as if the return exceeded the wager. One anecdote is worth describing here. Years ago, I was conducting a study that was designed to investigate the role of endorphins, naturally occurring brain substances mimicking the effects of morphine, in producing 'highs' associated with gambling. Two subjects, having placed a bet, returned to the laboratory where an intravenous catheter was inserted into their arms to draw blood samples and their heart rate was recorded while they listened to the race broadcast. During the broadcast, one subject's responses showed a marked increase as expected, but I was puzzled to find no increase in arousal in the other. When I questioned him, he informed me that the horse he had selected was a last-minute withdrawal and that he in fact had no bet resting on the outcome. While he listened with interest to the broadcast, he was not excited to anywhere near the same extent as his companion; the bet made all the difference.

Others are unable to consider ceasing gambling because they become totally immersed in the activity to the exclusion of all other thoughts. All the sources of stress in their lives fade into the background as their focus of attention is narrowed on the task at hand: the act of gambling and the thrill of pursuing the next bet. Under such circumstances, gambling becomes a useful platform on to which one can escape from current emotional hassles and the anxieties of daily life. Gambling can also serve to alleviate boredom and depressed mood states. Many gamblers describe a feeling of elation when engaged in the process of gambling and in anticipation of the outcome. They participate because gambling makes them feel positive and happy, particularly during the intervening period between betting and awaiting the results; here they feel a lift in mood as they anticipate and daydream about a positive outcome.

The motivation to cease gambling is often externally driven. It is true that a few gamblers are fully aware of their loss of control and realise that they must take action to prevent the development of significant problems in their lives. These people acknowledge that they are spending more time or money than they intended on gambling and that they have a sense of impaired control. They suffer a continual preoccupation with gambling and/or an inability to cease once they have commenced. Three-quarters of gamblers, however, are pressured to modify their behaviour by their spouses or partners, relatives or employers. These people are usually motivated by a desire to stop the gamblers developing significant problems in their lives, for example, marital tension, social isolation and loss of employment productivity, as a result of persistent losses. Gambling more than one can personally afford will result in some impact on one's quality of life. The impact can range from causing some level of discomfort through to severe distress. Having a poorer quality of life in itself may not prompt a person to seek assistance. The motivation to obtain help will often emerge once the impact causes psychological distress to either the gambler or family member. At this point, the gambler will (perhaps reluctantly) come to the realisation that something needs to be done to overcome the gambling urges and behaviours. Hopefully, this book will serve to motivate you to seek help before the distress, conflict and pain grows in intensity.

It is important to understand that some gamblers are reluctant to seek treatment because they believe that they can overcome their problems on their own and consequently do not need outside help. It takes courage to ask for help but that courage reflects a belief in your own strength to take steps and gain benefit. Asking for guidance is not a weakness or admission of failure; quite the contrary, it shows strength of character.

Similarly, the stigma associated with gambling is another deterrent to seeking help. There is no shame in asking for assistance for a problem. Counsellors are non-judgmental and more than willing and able to offer constructive advice and therapy. The overall message is: do not hesitate to access counselling, and do so as soon as you feel any concerns about your gambling. The earlier you do so, the better the outcome.

Two principles of treatment

There are two main yet opposing principles of treatment proposed for problem gambling. In the first, the goal is 'abstinence'; in the second, it is 'controlled' gambling. Each will be discussed below. Gamblers Anonymous, as well as mental health and drug and alcohol treatment programmes, advocate complete abstinence as the essential goal of any therapeutic intervention. Applied to gambling, abstinence is taken to mean absolutely no participation in any form of gambling on any level; this includes the occasional and infrequent purchase of raffle, lottery or scratch tickets, as well as entry into draws or office sweepstakes. According to this principle, then, the effectiveness of a treatment is based on very strict criteria. Abstinence is considered essential because of the strongly held belief that any episode of gambling, no matter how slight, will inevitably result in a relapse and resumption of compulsive gambling patterns. This belief is the same as that held for alcoholism and is reflected in the dictum of Gamblers Anonymous that compulsive gambling is a chronic progressive disorder that can never be cured but only arrested.

However, using abstinence as the only criterion for success in treatment ignores such important indices of improvement as reduced frequency of gambling, intensity and urge to gamble; enhanced ability to control gambling once commenced; and improved social, interpersonal and financial functioning.

A detailed reading of the psychological and psychiatric literature reveals that many outcome studies refer to marked reduction in the frequency and intensity of gambling after treatment. Positive gains are made despite the presence of continued gambling at much reduced levels. This has led several researchers to evaluate the effectiveness of controlled gambling. 'Control' in this context is used to describe a situation in which the gambler can place defined bets according to prearranged or agreed limits. In one case, a 44-year-old man with a twenty-year history of excessive gambling maintained control for almost all of the two-year follow-up period. In all the cases reported, the gambler's spouse was involved in financial management and supervision.

In a follow-up study over periods of from two to nine years, it was found that a third of gamblers achieved controlled gambling over a period of on average five years following behavioural therapy. This group showed a reduction on measures of psychopathology, gambling expenditure and debt, and at the same time improvement in overall quality of life, marital relationships and self-esteem. Importantly, a number of abstinent gamblers reported one or two lapses that did not lead to relapse or to a resumption of continued gambling. These episodes were confined to brief periods, less intense in magnitude and easier to overcome.

Similarly, in a more recent five-year follow-up study conducted in Canada, results showed a very mixed pattern of gambling outcomes over time. Some individuals meeting criteria for a gambling disorder at the start of the five years did not meet criteria in subsequent years. The reverse pattern was shown for others. In essence, problem gambling shows an unstable pattern where the bulk of problem gamblers tend to experience problems for a period of a year or longer before these are resolved. The greater the severity of problem gambling, the more likely it is that the problems will persist for a longer time period, and that the gambler will relapse in later years. But the main findings are consistent with the clinical intervention studies: the majority of problem gamblers can and do overcome their problems and resume positive lives.

Should a gambler try for controlled gambling rather than abstinence to start off with in treatment? It can be argued that there are certain advantages in offering controlled gambling, particularly with those people who are poorly motivated or do not believe that they want to or are able to achieve the difficult task of giving up entirely. Offering controlled gambling may increase the chance that ambivalent gamblers:

- agree to seek treatment;
- enter treatment at an earlier stage in their career;
- accept treatment because they feel that that can reduce but not totally stop gambling;
- see control as a more realistic and achievable goal for themselves;
- don't drop out of treatment because of one or two lapses. With abstinence one lapse represents a failure, whereas with controlled gambling one lapse means that you have to apply control strategies more effectively.

A word of caution is in order here. While there is some suggestion that controlled gambling may be possible, at this stage we still do not know how to differentiate between those gamblers who can achieve control over their compulsive gambling habits and those who cannot. Nor do we know the factors that predict who will or will not resume compulsive gambling after a lapse. Therefore, it is imperative that gamblers accept the necessity of abstinence as the preferred objective in the first instance. Only once they demonstrate a capacity to eliminate their compulsive urges can they even begin to contemplate the notion of control. Even then, the advice must always be to avoid gambling. Why take the chance of exposing yourself to risk if you have already demonstrated a failure to retain control over behaviour in the past?

Gamblers have a tendency to rationalise and justify much of their behaviour. Cognitive distortions allow them to embark on a course of action that will eventually lead to their downfall – much in the same way as the alcoholic who convinces himself that he can visit his friends at the local pub without having a drink. He may be successful for a period but then succumb to the temptation, usually feeling sure at that point that he can have one or two drinks without losing control. It is important for gamblers to have a strategy for dealing with the risk of relapses.

How can relapses after treatment be prevented?

Once you have regained control over gambling, the battle is not completed. The trick is making sure that you do not slowly fall back into the trap. You cannot be complacent. This does not mean that you will always suffer the disorder of compulsive gambling for the rest of your life. Research has shown that some people can maintain controlled gambling over a long period of time; but, as discussed previously, this is not an advisable goal to aim for in the first instance. People have a tendency to fall back into old practices over time and mistakenly believe that they have conquered or cured the problem. All too often, gamblers say, 'I have not had the urge to gamble now for the last six months or so. I'm in control. Let's test it out. I'll just enter the gambling arena and see how I feel. One bet is all I'll have. There's no harm in that, surely.' What is happening here is the first step in a series of apparently irrelevant decisions that will invariably lead to a fall.

Relapse-prevention strategy has grown out of the study of addiction. Its main purpose is to teach people to see the chain of seemingly innocent links that gradually leads them to a high-risk situation where the likelihood of a relapse or 'bust' is greatly increased. One of the most important components of any treatment programme is learning how to avoid the pitfalls that are likely to result in long-term failure. Once you have identified the conditions under which you are most likely to experience the urge to gamble or the triggers that cause a rise in your interest and urge, as well as the alternative steps to take to change your course of action, and have learned how to seek support from others close to you, you are well on the way to continued long-term recovery.

In essence, what you need to do is to learn a number of straightforward strategies that will:

> - help you reduce your urge to gamble when it arises through a relaxation technique (imaginal desensitisation);
> - correct faulty logic and thinking processes that cause you to persist in the belief that you have special skills or control over the outcome of a chance event and that you can actually win at gambling over the longer term;

- learn to identify triggers that will provoke your urge to gamble in future, such as negative emotional states;
- learn stress management and problem-solving strategies that will give you alternative ways of dealing with stress, anxiety and depression;
- learn to avoid gambling-related cues that will fuel your desire to gamble.

Before moving on to the practical aspects of how to regain control over your gambling, we will next look briefly at some technical points related to problem gambling.

8

A short technical note

It is well known that people have gambled since ancient Egyptian times, but it was only at the beginning of the twentieth century that psychologists and psychiatrists first showed any interest in the behaviour. By the middle of the century, several treatments were being offered in self-help groups like Gamblers Anonymous or by psychologists and psychiatrists using behavioural and psychodynamic approaches, but it was not until 1975 and 1980 that problem gambling came to be accepted as a major psychiatric disorder when it was included in the International Classification of Diseases version 9, ICD- 9, and the American Psychiatric Association's classification system, the *Diagnostic and Statistical Manual of Mental Disorders*, third edition (known as DSM-III), respectively.

Remember, the terms used in these classification systems have varied over time: impulse control disorder, pathological gambling and, more recently, gambling disorder. These all really refer to the same condition, that is, someone who has difficulty controlling their gambling behaviour to affordable limits. So, be aware that we will be using one or more of these terms interchangeably; do not be confused because we are talking about the same conditions.

Gambling disorder: A disease or a social problem?

No one is really clear about the nature of a gambling disorder. The 'disease' model suggests that pathological gamblers are categorically distinct in some way from social gamblers and non-gamblers. This view is held by Gamblers Anonymous and health professionals who advocate classifying gambling as an addictive disorder. The opposing 'dimensional' approach argues that gambling lies on a continuum and that social and pathological gamblers represent extremes at each end of the spectrum. On this view, problem gambling is considered a social issue and not a psychological or psychiatric illness.

Although this debate continues, the American Psychiatric Association, in its *Diagnostic and Statistical Manual of Mental Disorders* (DSM-III, 1980, DSM-III_R, 1987, and DSM-IV, 1994), decided to regard gambling as a psychiatric condition but was not fully in favour of considering it a true addiction because there was no external substance involved. As a compromise, the decision was reached in DSM IV-TR (2000) to continue including pathological gambling in the category of 'Disorders of Impulse Control Not Elsewhere Classified' alongside a range of seemingly unrelated problems such as intermittent explosive personality, compulsive shoplifting (kleptomania), fire-setting (pyromania) and hair-pulling (trichotillomania). Importantly, however, the diagnostic criteria for pathological gambling were deliberately and directly based on those used for the substance abuse disorders.

In its most recent release, DSM-5 (2013) finally agreed to reclassify the condition as a behavioural addiction. It was relocated from the impulse control category to the Substance and Related Addictive Disorders category under the subclassification non-substance behavioural addictions. Although 'Internet condition' was mooted as another behavioural addiction, it was not included but mentioned as worthy of further study. In the meantime, only gambling disorder has been included in this category.

The defining features of a disorder of impulse control

There were three main features that distinguished disorders of impulse control in earlier diagnostic systems. These were (a) the repeated failure to resist an urge to carry out a behaviour that is (b) preceded by an increasing sense of tension and (c) results in an experience of pleasure, gratification or release following its completion. These features are also found in the group of sexual deviation disorders that includes exhibitionism (flashing), voyeurism (peeping Tom) and paedophilia (child sexual abuse), a separate and distinct group of behaviours that is also characterised by recurrent impaired control over urges.

In DSM-5, the condition was reclassified as a non-substance related addiction with some changes to the diagnostic criteria. The primary features are of the presence of persistent and repeated gambling that results in clinically significant distress or impairment. But remember when reading the criteria listed below that these are used to diagnose a disorder. Many gamblers who do not meet these diagnostic criteria do still experience gambling-related problems and require assistance. Do not discard this book or the notion that you might need counselling simply on the fact that you do not meet the number of items required for a diagnosis.

The definition of pathological gambling

A gambling disorder is defined as the presence of repeated gambling behaviour that leads to clinically significant negative consequences to the individual, family and/or community and society. In DSM-5, the condition is diagnosed when an individual meets four out of nine criterion items. These items cover behaviours that reflect the presence of an excessive pre-occupation with gambling, tolerance as shown by the need to gamble with increasing amounts, and withdrawal experienced as a state of restlessness or irritability in response to any attempt to stop or cut back gambling. Impaired control is identified by repeated unsuccessful attempts to reduce or stop gambling, and motivations are reflected in an item that determines if the individual is attempting to chase losses (that is, win back money already lost) and if the individual gambles when depressed or emotionally distressed. Other items refer to behaviour such as lying to conceal gambling, actions that compromise rela-tionships, employment or studies, and a reliance on others to provide assistance by providing money to pay debts.

In diagnosing the condition, it is important to rule out

any other psychiatric explanation – for example, a bipolar or psychotic (schizophrenia) disorder – that might be the main cause of excessive gambling. The condition may be described as occurring episodically or being persistently present, in remission or in persistent remission, and at a mild, moderate or severe level.

Two things need to be borne in mind. Firstly, the number of criteria required to obtain a diagnosis was reduced from five out of ten criterion items in DSM-IV to four out of nine in DSM-5. One item, committing an illegal act to obtain money to continue gambling, was discarded on the basis that it was not endorsed by many problem gamblers. This is somewhat controversial since a number of clinicians and researchers argue that this criterion item should be retained because it highlights severity. Importantly, some research has indicated that the changes made do not really affect the rates of diagnosing gambling disorders.

In addition, some further specifiers were included as indicated below; whether the condition is episodic or persistent, whether the condition is in remission and the severity of the condition.

As mentioned above, the criteria have been based deliberately on those for the substance abuse disorders. As noted, some of the times refer to tolerance, withdrawal symptoms and preoccupation or dependence. Some limited indications of withdrawal symptoms have been found in the handful of available studies that have shown that about a third of gamblers suffer headaches, gastrointestinal disturbances, irritability and sleeplessness in the period immediately after ceasing gambling. But more studies need to be carried out before it can be stated with any degree of confidence that withdrawal and tolerance are consistent features of problem gambling. For example, an individual may increase amounts gambled in an attempt to win larger amounts to repay mounting debts rather than to generate the same level of excitement. Despite this, gambling as an addictive disorder is generally accepted by counsellors, clinicians and researchers.

How common are gambling disorders?

Only a small proportion of adults can be said to suffer problem gambling. Substantially more people engage in responsible gambling. Surveys in the UK, Australia and the USA reveal that between 30 per cent and 90 per cent of adults have gambled at one time or other in their lives, depending on the availability of gambling outlets in the community. The varying rate across countries is determined by the degree to which religious beliefs (on the part of, for example, Muslims or Jehovah's Witnesses) or laws (in, for example, Hawaii compared to Nevada) specifically restrict or ban gambling.

Estimates suggest that 40 per cent gamble regularly, at least once a week. It can be stated that somewhere in the vicinity of 0.5–7.6 per cent of adults with an average of around 2.3 per cent gamble excessively, to the extent of meeting the formal diagnosis of a gambling disorder. An additional 1–3 per cent are said to fall in the domain of 'probable' problem gambling, that is, they show some but not all signs of a gambling disorder. Most pathological gamblers (about 75–85 per cent) are males, although data show a rising trend among females over the last ten years but stabilising to a ratio of six males to four females.

Where legal forms of gambling are available in the community, surveys reveal that 5–6 per cent of school-age adolescents meet the criteria for problem gambling. Indeed, 90 per cent of pathological gamblers report beginning in early adolescence, many starting to gamble as young as thirteen or fourteen years of age on non-commercial forms of gambling. While patterns vary considerably, with some gamblers becoming 'addicted' almost immediately after they first play, the general finding is that most are able to contain their gambling until their mid twenties before losing control; many do not seek treatment until about ten or so years later, in their late thirties. The average age at which treatment is sought is thirty-five to thirty-nine years. Note, however, that probably around nine out of ten individuals meeting criteria for a gambling disorder do not attend treatment. Some of these barriers include stigma and shame, belief that the gambling can be contained without outside assistance, not knowing where to obtain assistance and ambivalence about giving up gambling. These barriers to treatment can be overcome by accepting that there is no stigma or shame attached to seeking help, that help from others can be very effective in achieving control and that asking others (doctors, psychologists, telephone helplines or community health services) can direct you to services close by. All problem gamblers should be encouraged to use self-help guides and, importantly, to seek additional services from health professionals where necessary.

Pathological gambling, depression and substance abuse

Depression is commonly associated with problem gambling. About three-quarters of problem gamblers suffer severe depression, with about a fifth of these having serious suicidal thoughts or making a serious suicide attempt. A recent report by the Victorian Coroner's Court in Australia estimated that there was approximately one suicide per month that occurred in the context of gambling. The coroner's report also referred to co-morbid mental health problems being present, so the actual cause of the suicide may be complex. It could be that the gambling caused the depression, which led to suicide, or vice versa. In a proportion, the depression is present before gambling commences. In these instances, gambling is used as a means of alleviating the depression, in much the same way that an alcoholic may drink to reduce anxiety.

For many, the stress and strain of constant financial worry, pressure to make ends meet, and fear of spouses or partners, employers or the police finding out quickly takes its toll on mood and behaviour. The gambler becomes withdrawn, distant, moody and irritable. In most instances, severe depressive episodes, and in particular suicide attempts, occur following the disclosure or discovery of major financial debts and/or criminal activity. The shock of such revelations devastates the spouse or partner, who had until then remained totally unaware of any possible difficulties. The prospect of financial ruin, loss of assets including the home, legal action and loss of employment becomes emotionally overwhelming for all concerned. The loss of trust, intense anger and anxiety on the part of the spouse or partner results in arguments and the threat of separation or divorce.

During this crisis period, anti-depressant medication is often useful to help improve mood and reduce the risk of impulsive suicidal gestures. Consult your family doctor or local community mental health service for advice on these matters.

It is not surprising, then, that rates of alcohol abuse and/ or dependence in problem gamblers are high. Studies have repeatedly shown that approximately 20–30 per cent of problem gamblers show signs of excessive alcohol consumption. The precise pattern of association with actual gambling behaviour is unclear; alcohol is consumed either before, during or after gambling. Where it occurs beforehand, alcohol may act to impair judgment and weaken inhibitions against gambling. A typical story is that of the gambler who enters a bar to drink socially with his friends. His resolve not to gamble gradually reduces in strength and he decides to try his luck with a few pounds. Very soon he finds himself having lost all his money gambling and becomes remorseful, guilty and angry, promising never again to place himself in that situation. This promise is repeatedly made and broken. After a gambling episode, alcohol is consumed to deaden pain and emotional distress.

The services of a drug and alcohol counsellor in your local health facility are often useful in helping to break out of this unrelenting cycle.

The self-help programme outlined in Part Two of this book will help you regain control over your gambling habits. You may find it useful to supplement this by improving your own problem-solving and stress management skills and/or learning strategies to deal with depression by reading other self-help books in this series. Do consult your local family doctor or community mental health service for additional information on other treatment programmes.

PART TWO

A SELF-HELP COGNITIVE BEHAVIOURAL APPROACH TO OVERCOMING PROBLEM GAMBLING

Introduction

There are a number of strategies that can be used to assist the motivated person in overcoming problem gambling. How difficult it is to accomplish this task depends upon how much effort is put into the attempt. Some people are ambivalent about really wanting to give up an activity that they really enjoy, or that serves a psychological purpose in helping them to avoid confronting emotional difficulties. Some gamblers may believe that compulsive gambling is an incurable condition, or may simply not be aware that effective treatments exist. Others may not genuinely want to stop but feel coerced into trying in order to please their partners or employers. And yet it is clear that problem gambling can be overcome, if one really wants to, by following the steps outlined in the chapters to come.

An effective self-help approach

It is possible to overcome problem gambling by learning certain techniques and adopting more realistic attitudes and beliefs about the prospect of winning. For some, using the steps outlined in this self-help book is all that is needed; for others, the book may be best used in conjunction with more intensive treatment from a service offering special-ist counselling in problem gambling or from local mental health professionals. Either way, it is often advisable to attend Gamblers Anonymous meetings to obtain additional guidelines and support. Its sister organisation Gam-Anon is also a helpful source of support and information for spouses and partners of gamblers. Whichever path you take, this book can be the starting point for regaining control over your behaviour.

An important note

If you are in a crisis situation and likely to panic in such a way that you may harm yourself, immediately consult a psychiatrist or your local family doctor, who will provide necessary care for you. Once the crisis has resolved itself and you are no longer in danger of self-harm, you can proceed to use this book while continuing to receive professional help.

Who will benefit from this self-help book?

This book is intended primarily for people who are interested in regaining control over gambling urges and behaviour that create problems in their life. It is also a useful resource for family members who wish to have additional information that may aid them in offering assistance to the gambler. Broadly speaking, there are several groups who should find this book to be of benefit:

- Those whose gambling has become excessive and as a result is causing distress to themselves or others close to them. The distress may be associated with financial difficulties, depression and anxiety, marital strain, threatened employment or legal action. The level of distress may vary from feeling constantly unhappy and under pressure to deeply depressed and suicidal. For many, professional help must be sought. For them, this book can complement psychological treatment offered by professionals.

- Those who have ventured into problem gambling but are still at an early stage. These people have recognised the first warnings of danger – spending too much time or money gambling – but are not yet experiencing serious consequences. They may not need professional intervention at this stage and tend to respond extremely well to the instructions contained in this book. For them, this book can act as a preventive measure, saving them from economic and personal hardship.

- Those who move between controlled and problem gambling. A number of people are able to gamble socially for a period of time but then experience episodes where they go overboard and create problems. This book can teach them the skills necessary to recognise and limit the extent of their gambling when they begin to lose control.

- Those social gamblers who want to cut down their gambling to more acceptable levels. One does not have to have problems in order to benefit from this book! Some report no difficulty in controlling their behaviour except under certain circumstances. They complain that they occasionally have minor difficulties stopping once they start. This book contains hints on how to identify high-risk situations and take preventive action.

- Family members and relatives who are seeking information and guidance on how best to encourage and support their loved one in the attempt to overcome problem gambling. The general principles outlined in this book should provide comfort and reassurance.

Who should seek further assistance?

As noted above, not all people who cannot control their gambling will find fully adequate help in this book; some may need additional professional assistance. As a general guide, the types of people who may require special attention are as follows.

- Those for whom gambling is not the primary problem. In some psychiatric conditions such as bipolar disorder, schizophrenia or major depression, gambling is just one of several disordered behaviours present. In mania, for example, elevated euphoria and grandiose ideas lead to a sense of overconfidence in the possibility of winning, resulting in uncharacteristic or bizarre patterns of gambling behaviour, while the sense of hopelessness associated with depression may cause one not to care about excessive losses. Where there is a suggestion of an underlying psychiatric condition, seek professional care from a psychiatrist or clinical psychologist. Medication is often a necessary part of treatment. Once the primary condition is treated, the gambling behaviour may itself decrease spontaneously.

- Where suicide is a real threat – particularly where there is a combination of alcohol dependence and depression, and where there is a looming financial, legal or marital catastrophe. Here it is essential that proper medical attention be given to reduce the risk of self-harm as soon as possible. Teaching cognitive behavioural strategies to control gambling is temporarily set aside until the suicidal condition has stabilised. This book can be introduced once the risk of self-harm is contained and under proper professional supervision.

- Those who suffer from alcohol dependency. About a fifth to a third of alcoholics have a coexisting gambling problem, while a similar proportion of gamblers suffer from alcohol dependency. Alcohol can very easily impair one's judgment and self-control. If you suspect you may have a drinking problem, it is strongly recommended that you seek treatment from your local drug and alcohol services counsellor. Two to four standard drinks is the suggested daily limit for alcohol consumption. If you consume more than this, it is wise to obtain professional advice.

- Those who are heavily pressured by their partner, employer or solicitor to seek help to reduce their gambling. These gamblers are generally resentful and, although agreeing to read the book, fail to follow advice or apply the strategies outlined. In these circumstances motivation is low, compliance poor and, not surprisingly, success rare. For these people, the initial step must be individual sessions with a mental health professional aimed at motivating the gambler to stop. You cannot force change on an unwilling person, no matter how much you try. The best strategy is one of encouragement and support.

- A related group is those gamblers who flatly and consistently deny that they have a problem.

Constantly confronting them leads only to arguments and continued denial. These people are just not interested in receiving help. Again, encouragement and support, not pressure and threats, are the responses most likely to maximise the possibility of a change in attitude.

- Where gambling is an expression of resentment, hostility and anger toward a partner. In some cases, a person may gamble excessively to get back at his or her partner for something they have done. A wife who finds out her husband is having an affair may subconsciously accelerate her gambling to get even with him by spending their savings, for example. Here, it is important to identify the underlying reasons for gambling and obtain appropriate marital or relationship counselling. The book may assist in the process once the relationship conflicts are resolved.

- Those suffering brain injury or intellectual impairment. Brain damage or impairment may affect judgment, the degree to which behaviour can be inhibited and the consequences of actions taken understood. In this context, the book may provide excellent resource material to which the person can repeatedly refer; but it is necessary to make sure that the instructions are fully comprehended. Therefore, in these cases it may be useful to have a mental health professional familiar with brain or intellectual impairment guide the person through the steps outlined in the book.

Resistance to change

The steps set out in the following chapters are designed to help you overcome your gambling problem. What is meant by overcoming your problem depends on what goal you wish to pursue – to become completely abstinent and never gamble again, or to reduce your activity to acceptable levels. To commit yourself to giving up entirely can be a difficult decision to take.

To help you make your decision, list here some reasons in favour of and against giving up completely; now do the same for only reducing your level. This exercise helps you to evaluate the pros and cons of stopping or reducing your gambling. Hopefully this will motivate you to increase your efforts once you realise that your quality of life will improve as a result.

REASONS FOR:	
Giving up gambling altogether	Simply reducing your level
REASONS AGAINST:	
Giving up gambling altogether	Simply reducing your level

Whichever you choose, ultimately it means that you must give up or decrease an activity that may be highly exciting for you. This is a difficult choice, and one that some people try to resist for as long as possible. Excuses include that the problem is not really as bad as it seems, one will stop next week, or there is nothing comparable to replace the gambling. It is important to accept that gambling is creating hazards in your life, producing stress and affecting the happiness of your family. Your quality of life is poorer for it. The longer you delay, the deeper will be the hole you have dug for yourself out of which you have to climb. Keep in mind that the quality of your life will be vastly improved if you accept the challenge of overcoming your gambling.

Preparing for change

Sometimes there are a number of additional problems that need to be dealt with before the process of change outlined in this book can be commenced. These are obstacles in the way of taking that difficult first step toward self-help.

Current financial problems

Most gamblers are in debt. Often the true level of debt is kept concealed from others. Part of the anxiety and pressure to gamble derives from the wish to win enough to repay debts before anyone finds out. The difference between a positive and a negative response to treatment often rests on how prepared one is to be open and honest with one's partner in revealing the full extent of existing debts. You will need to trust your partner that even though they may react with anger, they will respect you for coming clean. It is the lies, deceit and uncertainty that cause so much distress and suffering to partners.

The best thing to do, then, is to face the problem head-on and in full:

- Make a tally of all debts, whether owed to friends, banks, loan companies or credit card companies.
- Give your partner the details of all your debts.
- Do not try to conceal any debt. This only creates distrust later on when found out.
- Tell your partner that you wish to take full responsibility for repaying all debts.
- Arrange to have your pay deposited directly into your bank account.
- Ask your partner to help you work out a budget plan. Calculate your regular weekly income and expenditure. Put aside enough out of your income to pay all regular bills. Where possible, arrange direct automatic payments out of your account.
- Plan to pay off debts over time rather than immediately. Keep in mind that rushing to pay off debts only serves to make you think of returning to gambling as a quick-fix solution. It won't work.
- Involve your partner as a support in helping you deal with your problem.

Terry was nine thousand pounds in debt. He panicked because he believed it would take him years to repay it. The thought of working hard just to give his earnings to someone else (in repaying debts) frustrated him. He felt he was getting nowhere. One large win would do the trick, he hoped. But the debt increased with each passing week. When he introduced a sensible budget designed to cover living costs and pay off part of his debt regularly, he was surprised to discover that it took only eighteen months to eliminate his debt completely. Seeing his debts slowly decreasing encouraged him enormously.

Sometimes it may be necessary to consult an accountant or financial advisory support service to obtain advice on how to plan a budget. These services will review your income and expenditure and work out the most efficient approach to managing your finances. Often, it is easier and cheaper to take out one loan to repay all outstanding debts rather than have multiple debts at high interest rates. An additional advantage of making use of these services is that they can negotiate with financial institutions to vary the terms of your loans to make them more manageable.

Receiving financial guidance is beneficial in giving one a sense of structure and control over a seemingly chaotic situation. Seeing a light at the end of the tunnel will increase your hope, confidence and motivation in overcoming gambling.

Legal problems

Even though it is no longer included in the diagnostic criteria, a large number of gamblers commit offences as a means to supplement their gambling funds. This happens when they are no longer able to borrow money from legitimate sources. In the desperation phase, stealing petty cash, writing cheques with insufficient funds in the account and even forging signatures are common. In extreme cases, gamblers may engage in large-scale embezzlement or selling drugs, as I have seen on several occasions. I have now treated more than half a dozen clients who have taken in excess of a million Australian dollars from their employers. In one sad case, a 21-year-old university student accessed his accountant father's trust account held for clients. Over two years he lost just over a million dollars of his father's clients' accounts, resulting in a criminal charge against the student and the loss of his father's accountancy business. An extreme case but illustrative of the extent of harm that can be produced.

For most gamblers, the slide into crime is gradual and unintentional. One small crime leads to another until finally they are in such dire straits that they believe that more gambling is the only path to salvation. Do not fall into this trap.

One fortunate client I saw recognised the danger signs and acted promptly to avoid the looming anguish. Jack, a 46-year-old hardware delivery driver, regularly collected cash from customers. He was in the habit of banking sales proceeds at the close of the day. One Friday, he was running late and missed the bank. He decided to keep the money over the weekend and deposit it first thing Monday morning. During the Saturday, he was given a sure tip on a horse. Not having his own cash available, he decided to take a hundred pounds out of the money that needed to be banked. He did not realise that this is an illegal act. The horse lost – not by much, but that didn't make any difference. His employer's money was gone. He contemplated taking the remainder to see if he could win back the losses. Sensibly he resisted, told his boss on Monday morning what had happened and agreed to a plan to repay the money. His employer then introduced a new set of guidelines for delivery drivers to prevent a similar circumstance from recurring and to take any further temptation away from Jack. Had Jack not made that decision to confess, I am sure that his situation would have deteriorated to the extent of possible police action being taken against him.

One needs to be aware that problem gambling is not a defence for diminished responsibility at law. In committing a crime, one is aware that what one is doing is wrong, and that one has full control over one's behaviour. The strong urge is to gamble, not to commit a crime. In the same way, a heroin addiction is no excuse for committing a crime.

If you are committing offences to support your habit:

* Stop any further offences immediately. Ask yourself: Where will it lead? How long will it be before I get caught?
* Unburden yourself by discussing your actions

with your partner. Once over the shock, a partner may provide good advice, help you make sensible decisions and offer strong support in dealing with the problem.

- Consider restitution and informing your employer. You need to repay all monies taken.
- Seek legal advice. If you have committed a major offence, do not continue in the hope of winning enough to cover your tracks and conceal the crime.
- Take responsibility for your actions. Even though it is an extremely difficult decision to take, accept the consequences of what you have done with the guidance of a solicitor. The alternative is living constantly in fear of discovery. Many a client suffers chronic anxiety, becoming jumpy and agitated every time the phone rings or a car pulls up outside their home. They report that when finally apprehended, a sense of relief is experienced: 'It is as though a weight has been lifted off my shoulders.'

Substance abuse

Gambling and substance abuse is a deadly combination. It aggravates existing problems and contributes to a worsening of depression, anxiety and low self-esteem.

Many gamblers turn to alcohol and drugs (both prescription medications and illicit drugs) to cope with stress and deaden the pain of guilt. Apart from the physical ill-effects of substance abuse, one's ability to think clearly and consider the consequences of actions is grossly impaired. Alcohol also reduces one's motivation and interferes with recovery. The will to resist urges is weakened, making a relapse more likely.

If you consume alcohol:

- Do not drink before or while you gamble.
- Avoid drowning your sorrows in drink after losing. Talk to your partner instead.
- If you are dependent, or others complain of your drinking, consult your local family doctor or community drug and alcohol service.
- If you are in a crisis and depressed, seek help immediately; do not rely on alcohol to see you through the day. Alcohol may increase the risk of self-harm in a moment of despondency and impaired judgment.

Marital problems

Financial strain is a notorious cause of marital friction. Gamblers spend considerable time away from home, and when there are constantly moody and irritable with members of their family. Constant criticism and pressure from a partner to 'do something about your problem' merely aggravate the tension within the family. In couples where arguments are frequent and either partner is repeatedly having their inadequacies or past broken promises thrown in their face, they feel put down, unsupported and unvalued. Gambling is seen as a refuge from this situation and a way of dealing with the negative emotions.

If you are experiencing marital strain, it is wise to consult a relationship or marital counsellor at your local community health service. It is essential that you and your partner work in cooperation.

Gamblers often excel in shifting blame for their behaviour on to others. Some common thought processes include:

- I gamble because my partner doesn't understand me.
- I gamble because my partner does not pay me enough attention.
- My partner's constant criticism or nagging forces me to gamble.
- My partner is no longer sexually attracted to me so I turn to gambling to make me feel better.
- My partner always wants things that I can't afford, so I gamble to try to win the money to buy them.

> • My partner is always pestering me to do things,
> so I gamble to get away for peace and quiet.

The essential point to remember is that it is the gambler's choice to gamble: no one else's. No partner should feel guilty for being the so-called cause of their partner's gambling behaviour.

Why do I have a problem gambling and not others?

True, most people are able to gamble socially without going overboard and getting into trouble. Some gamble excessively on occasion, that is, until they hit a certain level when they pull back. Some regular gamblers have a run of bad luck but are still able to contain their problems. Various possible explanations have been put forward as to why some people lose control and gamble excessively and others do not, but at present no one really knows. Reasons suggested by clinicians and researchers can be broken down into three broad categories: learnt behavioural habits, an addictive condition or an emotional response. One or a combination of these factors may contribute to loss of control.

Learnt behaviour habits

A person may develop a habit through exposure to gambling

and the excitement generated by winning. With repeated exposure, the habit strengthens and becomes part of one's lifestyle. Following a bout of losses that one can ill afford, attempts are made to recover the amount lost. Thus begins the process of chasing losses and the inevitable downward cycle into debt. At this point, problems develop and one has difficulty stopping. This process is often reinforced by the presence of errors in thinking and in understanding of the mathematics and operation of various gambling forms. A typical belief is that one can recoup one's losses by continued gambling. This is illogical given that gambling has caused the problems in the first instance; continued gambling will do little other than aggravate the problem.

An addictive condition

This is an increasingly accepted conception of gambling held by many clinicians and Gamblers Anonymous. It is a compelling view of gambling because of the many similarities with substance addiction. More recent work in genetics and in the neurosciences has provided evidence of a family link in gambling potentially related to a vulnerability to respond differently to reward and punishment compared to non-problem gamblers. It is not clear what genes precisely are involved, no doubt multiple genes, but it does appear that these increase the likelihood of someone becoming addicted to a substance or behaviour. Similarly, brain imaging studies have shown differences in activities in the regions controlling reward and decision-making. But although these differences may increase the propensity or risk of one becoming addicted, it does not mean that control over behaviour or responsibility for one's actions are lost. Rather, it makes it difficult but not impossible to control urges. One cannot excuse excessive behaviours that lead to harm by saying that 'my brain made me do it'. While there are similarities, there are also many differences. In essence, some of the effective strategies applied in the treatment of addictions can be usefully applied in overcoming problem gambling: for example, the principles of relapse prevention established in the treatment of addictions form a strong therapeutic foundation for overcoming problem gambling. The main point to accept is that one is not suffering a disease over which one has no control. One cannot dismiss responsibility for one's gambling behaviour by claiming one has an addiction.

Emotional response

Stress, anxiety, depression and other negative emotional states may cause a person to increase gambling behaviour. For these people, gambling serves as an emotional outlet or escape, or a means of avoiding having to deal with conflicts. They literally bury their heads in gambling. Poor stress management and/or problem-solving skills are a significant contributing factor to low mood and lack of self-esteem.

Irrespective of what you consider has contributed to the problem behaviour in your case, there are strategies and techniques you can learn and follow that will help you overcome your gambling problems. Through improvement in your sense of self-control and self-esteem after learning the skills outlined in the following chapters, your quality of life will be considerably enhanced.

About the self-help programme

The self-help guidelines set out in this book are designed to provide you with the necessary skills to regain control over your problem gambling behaviour. The foundation of the programme is the relaxation-based imaginal desensitisation technique that several years of clinical research have shown to be highly effective in reducing compulsive and problem gambling habits. However, this skill is not learnt in isolation. Strategies designed to enable you to challenge your attitudes and beliefs about gambling and to identify and deal with high-risk situations are also described in some detail.

Not everything in this book will be of equal benefit to everyone. It is important to pick out those components which best apply to each individual's circumstances and to use those to maximum benefit. It is necessary to read and re-read steps over a period of time to refresh your memory and sharpen up your skills. Each time you read the book, you may find something else to boost you along the road to recovery. It is important to use this book as a resource guide, referring to it whenever an occasion arises when there may be a risk, no matter how trivial it may seem, of a lapse looming ahead.

As with any learnt skill, it takes time and practice for successful results to be achieved. Overcoming ingrained habits and learning new habits does not occur overnight, so do not expect instantaneous results. A measured pace over time achieves the best results.

How this self-help book should be used

Read the book through once completely to get a general sense of what is required. Then go back to the beginning with the idea of taking one step at a time. Do not rush or skim the material, as you may miss important suggestions. It will take about one week for you to become familiar with the relaxation-based imaginal desensitisation technique. After that, learning to identify irrational beliefs and ways to challenge these can take anywhere from one or two weeks to a month or so. There is no strict timetable; each person can and should work at his or her own pace. What is important is to work through the steps systematically and to revise steps at regular intervals. Do not become despondent if you do not respond immediately; it takes time and effort to get results. Progress is not necessarily smooth, so expect some setbacks as you go along. Learn from these by referring to the book and reviewing ways of handling these situations more effectively should they arise again in the future.

As you work slowly through each section, it is advisable to jot down your thoughts and ideas on paper, or on your tablet/smartphone. Having something in writing allows you to compare notes to see how you are faring over time. Also, and importantly, it gives you the opportunity of showing others your thoughts about gambling. Feedback from others is a very useful way of challenging irrational thoughts and gaining suggestions on how to correct them.

Step 3 below involves the suggestion of recording, via a recording device, a series of habitual gambling practices and relaxation instructions that are read out aloud. Take time to do the recording and recruit the assistance of a partner to help supervise your practice session. Knowing that someone is monitoring practice sessions is a good way of maintaining motivation and momentum. Do not be afraid to discuss your concerns with the person offering supervision. He or she can provide alternative suggestions or pick up on irrational thinking styles. In addition, he or she can acknowledge successes and significant achievements that you may overlook. Do not underestimate the importance of external praise in reinforcing your motivation and keeping up the impetus toward recovery.

As time goes on, you can become increasingly independent in recognising danger signals and applying the skills you have learnt to continue on the road to recovery. The ultimate aim of this book is to teach you lifelong skills in controlling your behaviour.

An overview of the programme

The book is set out systematically with each step providing exercises to follow, tasks to complete and techniques to practise.

Step 1: Understanding and improving your motivation to stop or reduce your gambling; establishing outcome goals

In Step 1 you will evaluate why you are setting out to overcome your problem gambling. This is to make sure that your motivation is governed by the right reasons, that is, that you are embarking on this self-help programme for your own benefit and not to please others. It is essential that your motivation stems personally from within and that you are fully committed to change. Change comes from within, and cannot be imposed on you by others. Family members can be supportive but they cannot force you to change unless you understand their concerns and cooperate in trying to achieve a common goal or goals.

Step 2: Monitoring your level of gambling

Step 2 outlines a way in which you can record how much gambling takes place daily. The purpose of this step is to enable you to realise exactly how much time and money you spend gambling and to identify links between emotions and cues in your environment that trigger your urge. A review of monitoring sheets at regular intervals helps plot your progress and show you how much you have achieved over time. This can encourage you to keep going during shaky times. In monitoring exactly how much you gamble, remember, do not react to the realisation of how much you have lost by increasing your gambling. Be aware that losses will not be regained by further gambling. Doing so will only worsen your situation. Accept the losses and look toward other ways of reducing your financial problems.

Step 3: Learning a relaxation-based skill to enable you to overcome the urge to gamble; learning to identify triggers and situations that trigger lapses

A practical skill with which you can counter urges as soon as they appear is taught in Step 3. This is a powerful procedure that lowers the drive to gamble to a manageable level. Understanding the types of stresses and cues in the environment that remind you of gambling and learning how to tackle the tension and excitement generated by them can build your self-esteem and confidence. Instead of becoming physically tense or excited when thoughts of gambling enter your mind, with the relaxation procedure you can foster a sense of calm and control.

Step 4: Controlling gambling-related cues

Urges and cravings to gamble are often triggered by cues associated with gambling – for example, walking past a sign advertising gambling, seeing a TV advertisement or listening to friends talking about their bets. This is because these cues remind you of previous wins and/or cause you to think that you can do so again on this occasion. One way of preventing urges and cravings from being triggered is to avoid, as much as you can, situations associated with gambling or that make gambling possible. This is often very difficult to do as it may mean travelling along a different route home to avoid walking past a betting shop or hotel, not reading the newspaper's sports section or listening to race broadcasts, blocking pop-ups from gambling sites on the computer/smartphone/tablet, not carrying additional cash on you and leaving your debit/credit cards at home. Avoiding things that will tempt you to think about gambling or trigger urges to gamble is easier than dealing with those urges and cravings.

Step 5: Identifying and challenging irrational thoughts and beliefs related to gambling

Step 5 examines how irrational thoughts and distorted ways of thinking about gambling contribute to problem gambling behaviour. There is little doubt that false beliefs about gambling being a source of income or opportunity to improve one's financial situation contribute to repeatedly bringing one back to try again. There are indeed many false and mistaken beliefs held about gambling. Challenging one's view about gambling, coming to understand the true reason underlying one's motivation to gamble and recognising what the activity is really all about can radically alter one's desire to continue gambling.

Step 6: Preventing future episodes

Step 6 teaches strategies to use in recognising danger signals and identifying high-risk situations. Knowing when a lapse is about to happen enables one to short-circuit the process by taking appropriate decisive action. Changing lifestyle patterns to minimise contact with cues associated with gambling and learning adequate problem-solving skills is a good way of ensuring that the positive gains achieved will be maintained. It is important to understand how stress, low mood and anxiety can trigger the urge to begin gambling again as a way of coping with these feelings. Temporary relief that leads to longer-term harms is no solution. Learning ways of coping with these in the first instance is more productive and will avoid future pain.

Step 7: Eliciting family support

Finally, overcoming gambling is made easier when family members provide strong support and encouragement. Working in cooperation with others is one excellent way of improving marital and family relationships, as well as a source of strength in boosting commitment to change and maintaining momentum. The trustfulness and quality of one's relationships are vastly improved as a result of open communication.

A review section is provided at the end of each step to help prompt you and to act as a reminder when you return to the book for revision. It is recommended that you re-read various sections and refresh your skills as time goes on.

Some reflections on gambling in general

At this point it may be useful to pause and offer some comments on the general nature of gambling and the principles applied in this book. There is nothing intrinsically good or bad about gambling. The negative factors associated with gambling come from faulty practices that lead to problems in various areas of one's life. The majority of people gamble sensibly and view the activity as a form of entertainment and fun. As is frequently stated, while these people hope to win, they really expect to lose. The amount they lose is limited and well within their means. For others, however, gambling gets out of hand and problems quickly follow.

Now, while for some people the only way to recover is by complete avoidance of any gambling, for others it is perfectly possible to resume the activity at controlled levels. It is important to understand that what works for one person is ineffective for another. So you must choose what you personally want to achieve from this book in terms of abstinence or controlled gambling. But take care when considering this that you are not merely deluding yourself into thinking you can continue controlled gambling when it is apparent that you will only repeat a previous cycle of failed attempts.

While many suggestions offered can be of benefit, do not think that everything contained in this book will work for you, or you may be disappointed. Pick out and practise those that produce results for you.

One final word. There may be others among your friends or colleagues who you may come to consider suffer from a similar condition of problem gambling. Resist the temptation constantly to badger them to do something about their problem or to parade your successes in overcoming problem gambling. Rather, gently offer them support and encouragement by informing them of resources such as this book to which they can turn for assistance. Give them time and space to come to terms with their need to seek help.

I cannot begin to tell you how my life has changed for the better. I am no longer obsessed with thoughts of where my next pound will come from, plagued by fears that my boss will find out how much time from work I have lost, or worrying about my wife's reaction when she finds out once again I haven't paid the bills. Now, whenever I have the urge, which is rare these days, I just take two minutes time out, relax and imagine myself walking away without having given in. If the urge persists, I think of how I am going to feel after I finish betting and coming out a loser. The operators are the only real winners in this game. That really turns me off gambling. The best thing about it is that for the first time in a long while, I have money in my pocket to spend on my wife and family. You should see the look on my kid's face when I come home with a present or tell him we're going out to the movies and for dinner. For once I have respect for myself. And so does my wife. Gee, it makes me feel like I'm floating on cloud nine. I should have come to my senses and stopped gambling ages ago.

Alan

Keep in mind the many benefits awaiting you from overcoming problem gambling. While you are making this decision for yourself, your partner, family and others you care about will also reap the rewards of your effort. It will also assist in repairing any feelings of helplessness, hopelessness, anger and/or loss of trust experienced by close family members. The path to recovery is not always smooth, nor is progress along it as quick as you may expect. You must not be surprised to experience temporary setbacks on the way. However much you may feel like throwing in the towel on these occasions, it is important not to become despondent. Rather, turn them around so that you use them as an exercise in learning to help you deal more effectively with similar events in the future. A positive attitude and consistent effort will eventually pay dividends. Look forward to an improved quality of life and the enhanced self-esteem that overcoming your gambling problem will produce for you.

Step 1

Working out your motivation to stop

A state coroner investigated the death of Mr M. S. In June, 1994 the Coroner reported that Mr M.S. was found in his motor vehicle parked at the local primary school. A hose attached to the exhaust pipe led to the inside of the vehicle. The Coroner's investigation indicated that the deceased suffered a compulsive gambling problem and had financial and marital problems. Earlier that year, the deceased appeared to be in an emotional and unstable state and had attempted suicide by taking an overdose. However, he refused to seek counselling for his problems around that time.

Victorian State Coroner, Australia, 1995

In 2011, the state coroner investigated the death of Mr B. C. The deceased was found hanging from the ceiling of his garage shortly after having played electronic gaming machines. Evidence indicated that he had made multiple cash withdrawals from the venue's ATM resulting in his losing the previous week's wage and leaving little money in his account. The Coroner concluded that the deceased suffered a gambling problem and a depressive disorder for which he was seeing his local doctor and psychologist for treatment. There was a known history of repeated borrowings of money from family and friends, and that he had a history of attending Gamblers Anonymous.

Victorian State Coroner, Australia, 2011

These two cases highlight the complexities of trying to understand the motivations why some people fail to seek treatment and others fail to respond to treatment.

Why was Mr M. S. not motivated to seek treatment? Did he believe that he did not have a problem, fail to recognise it or decide to try to resolve the problem himself with devastating effects?

Why was Mr B. C. motivated to overcome his gambling problem, seek help yet continue gambling? Was treatment ineffective or did his motivation change in response to his mood or external circumstances? Did his depression undermine his determination to control his gambling, or was it a trigger? Or, like many gamblers, was he ambivalent about ceasing his gambling? Although we will never know in Mr B. C.'s case, it does highlight the potential that some gamblers may seek treatment but unfortunately and tragically find it to be ineffective for a variety of reasons.

On the other hand, for others like Mr M. S. it may be that they are not prepared or ready to undergo a major change such as giving up gambling. Even if they are and do attend counselling, motivations can change rapidly, affecting their resolve to persist. Therefore, it becomes important to understand the role that motivation plays in overcoming gambling, even during therapy or with family support, and how fragile such motivations may be at times.

In general, willingness to seek and remain in treatment is based on individual beliefs, attitudes and prior experiences. Two psychologists, James Prochaska and Carlo DiClemente, have offered a useful framework for people to determine their position on a spectrum of readiness for change.

No awareness or reluctance to acknowledge the problem.
(Denial leading to a lack of motivation to change.)

⇓

Thinking about changing.
(Recognising a problem but still not actively motivated to change.)

⇓

Becoming determined to change.
(Gaining motivation and strength actually to do something to change.)

⇓

Taking active steps to start changing.
(Motivated to commence actively changing.)

⇓

Maintaining changes once they are made.
(Motivated to continue changes made.)

To begin with, no one can stop you from gambling. No change will occur if you choose to deny that a problem with gambling exists or if you pretend it does just to please others. Gaining motivation to change is the crucial first step toward recovery.

The desire to improve yourself must come from within, so it is important for you to understand the reasons why you are trying to give up gambling. If you are committed to improve for your own sake, then you will achieve your goals. If you are ambivalent, that is, you feel others are forcing you to give up but you would rather keep gambling given the opportunity, you are less likely to stop. However, if this is your situation, don't turn away from the possibility of improvement straight away; many gamblers have made great progress from apparently unpromising beginnings.

Even though excessive gambling causes personal distress, we know that many gamblers do not voluntarily seek help. In fact, most are pushed into it by people who are concerned by their self-destructive behaviour. Not surprisingly, a move to seek help is usually triggered by a major crisis caused by gambling. The crisis may be financial, when the expenses of daily living cannot be met, there is no money left to pay the rent or creditors are constantly calling for repayments on loans. Or it may involve problems within a relationship: there may be a threat of divorce because too much time is spent away from home or there is never enough money for the children or family/partnership activities. There may be legal reasons, as when a solicitor has advised therapy to give a good impression to magistrates before being sentenced for a gambling-related crime; or an employer may have suggested it because of poor work performance.

We have treated gamblers who are clearly not motivated but are undergoing therapy to satisfy the demands of their spouses. During treatment, and for reasons we do not understand, attitudes suddenly change in a positive direction. The principle should be, then, that even if on the surface the gambler does not seem motivated to change, treatment should be encouraged. So even an unmotivated gambler may benefit from reading this self-help guide!

Generally, however, any ambivalence on your part will lead to poor compliance with instructions and resistance to therapy. Ambivalence is a normal state of mind where there is a conflict in giving up something that is intrinsically reinforcing but also capable of producing harm. It is one reason that motivation can fluctuate in response to mood and external events and stresses. It is a fundamental understanding in clinical psychology and psychiatry that people do not change behaviour unless they are fully motivated. If coerced into therapy, there is a risk that you will simply 'go through the motions' of following instructions just to please others. The outcome will be that you will give the impression of doing well when in fact the problem is continuing behind people's backs – and your own.

There is no benefit in fooling yourself that you really want to stop when you don't. You will deny that you have any urge to gamble or that you have placed any bets. This will lull others into a false sense of security until they discover evidence of your gambling. Then, once again, you will have undermined people's trust in you.

Understanding your motivation

So how do you know when you are genuine in wishing to stop your problem gambling? What causes you to become motivated to seek treatment? It may be the realisation that you have hit 'rock bottom' and therefore need to change dramatically to save your marriage, coming close to suicide, public disclosure that finally lifts a 'weight off your shoulders' or you may have just become sick of a behaviour that constantly causes stress.

The first step you need to take is to be open and honest with yourself. To do this, it is very helpful to make a list of the reasons why you feel you should give up gambling. For example:

> - I am always struggling to keep up with payments for the home.
> - I never spend any time with my wife and children.
> - I am always lying to cover up.
> - I never have enough money to buy things for my family or myself.

Write down up to ten main reasons why you should stop gambling. Now rank them on a ten-point scale according to how important they are for you. Give the most important a rating of 1 and the least important a rating of 10.

	Reason	Ranking
1		
2		
3		
4		
5		
6		
7		
8		
9		
10		

Now compare these with any arguments you can think of as to why you should continue. Write down ten reasons in favour of why you think you should continue gambling.

For example:

- I believe I can win enough money to cover all my debts.
- I get a real sense of enjoyment out of gambling.
- Gambling is a way of escaping from my worries and problems.

As in the exercise before, rank them on a ten-point scale according to how important they are for you. Give the most important a rating of 1 and the least important a rating of 10.

	Reason	Ranking
1		
2		
3		
4		
5		
6		
7		
8		
9		
10		

Now take a few minutes to compare the two lists. Are most of the reasons given for continuing to gamble based on your desire to satisfy your own needs over and above anyone else's? As an exercise, recall the last time you won some money. Were you keen to put the cash aside so that you could gamble again the next day or did you immediately pay some outstanding bills? Now reverse the situation. When it comes to your partner putting money aside or buying personal items for her/himself, is your reaction different? Do you feel irritated and angry because you now have to spend your gambling kitty on rent or food? I'm sure you would agree that most problem gamblers like yourself keep the money for themselves and selfishly feel extremely resentful if they have to spend it on essential domestic purchases.

People who are highly motivated to overcome their gambling want to stop because:

- they have come to realise their behaviour is affecting not only themselves but also those who are close to them;
- gambling is causing major problems in all aspects of their life;
- they recognise that their desire to gamble is entirely for selfish reasons;
- life would be less emotionally draining if they stopped gambling.

The goal: Abstinence or controlled gambling?

A good way of testing your motivation is to consider what your overall aim is from this self-help book. Are you aiming to remain abstinent from gambling or do you wish to pursue controlled gambling?

Abstinence means that you will not gamble in any form, even soft forms such as raffles or office sweepstakes. Controlled gambling means that you will set limits on the amount and time you spend gambling each week. For example, you may set the limit at five pounds a week. Any wins are not re-gambled during the week but are put aside into a separate account. If you lose your five pounds early in the week, you do not take out any more money. You have to wait until your next allocation at the start of the next week. In this way, your maximum bet can only be five pounds over any week, irrespective of how much you are ahead.

Tick the box that best describes your self-help aim:

	Yes	No
Abstinence	☐	☐
Controlled gambling	☐	☐

If you have chosen controlled gambling, you will need to specify how much time and money you can afford each week:

Amount of money per week .... pounds

Amount of time per week .... hours

If you chose controlled gambling, seriously reconsider your motivation to overcome your problem gambling. Controlled gambling is an attractive aim; it allows you to justify continued indulgence in gambling while simultaneously reducing the pressure being placed on you by others to stop altogether. While it is true that a proportion of people can resume controlled gambling, we are still unable to predict with any degree of accuracy for whom this solution will work and for whom it will not.

Controlled gambling is hard to maintain because of the ease with which loss of control can occur. Frequent exposure to gambling cues, occasional wins and external stresses are all factors that act to apply pressure on you to escalate your level of involvement. The probability is that it is just a matter of time until you resume problem gambling habits again.

Take the example of Annabelle, a 45-year-old single mother living with a long-term partner.

I went to the club by myself to play the slot machines. I told myself that I would only spend the ten pounds, which was

my weekly gambling kitty. After a short while, I had the machine up to seventy-five pounds credit, but I wouldn't take the money out. Thought of what I would do with the money, buy Christmas presents. Blew the lot, I did. Feel sick now, depressed, disgusted with myself. I would have won a hundred pounds, was only at the club for an hour and a half. Walked out convinced I would never gamble again. In a bad mood all day. I'm not meant to have money, I run around all week with nothing in my purse. Imagine, I could have walked out with a hundred pounds, now nothing again. Why do I do this?

Two days later, Annabelle returned.

My downfall was thinking I could win back that hundred pounds. Blew all my money. Came home, gorged myself with food and felt worthless. Depressed and feeling very sick, physically and mentally. Where will I get the money to live on for the rest of the week? Gee, the only thing left to do is to borrow money from Jack and see if my luck changes. Can I really afford to stop now?

She was back on the merry-go-round of chasing losses.

In psychological treatment programmes, health professionals may recommend controlled gambling for those gamblers who refuse therapy because they do not want to give up totally or would refuse therapy because they believed it impossible to stop totally. It is considered important to encourage these people to start therapy whatever the aim. With assistance and the benefit of their own experience over time, they can come round toward more realistic expectations.

If you have selected controlled gambling as your goal at this point, it is essential that you involve your partner, friend or boss as a supervisor, that is, someone to whom you report. His/her role will be to monitor your level of gambling each week. It is also advisable to consult a health professional who will act as an additional external supervisor. Discussing your expectations with your partner is extremely important because it will help you work out exactly how much you can afford to gamble each week relative to your income and debts. It will also help you realise how much time away from other personal and family obligations will be spent on gambling.

If you want to pursue controlled gambling but are reluctant to be monitored by a supervisor, then you need to review your motivation. To argue that you can monitor progress on your own without the need to be under surveillance is to show misplaced confidence or – more probably – a wish to avoid responsibility. Go back to the beginning of Step 1 and re-evaluate your motivation.

Remember, the crucial step in gaining the most from this book is fully to understand your motivation. If you are uncertain, discuss the matter with your local counsellor or psychologist.

Others motivating a gambler to seek help

What should a partner do with a gambler who is reluctant to receive help? There is no one answer, but a number of suggestions can be offered as a guide:

- Resist constant nagging to go for help. Nagging raises tension and causes the gambler to dig his/ her heels in refusing.
- Refrain from making appointments on behalf of the gambler with health professionals. This is his/her responsibility. Gamblers seek the easy way out and given the chance will throw responsibility for action on to others.
- Provide written material informing him or her as to what help is available and where.
- Take steps to protect yourself from any debts that the gambler may incur. Seek legal advice in respect of joint accounts.
- Take steps to distance yourself from any responsibility for the gambler's debts. You may need to obtain legal advice.
- Avoid conspiring with the gambler to keep the gambling problem hidden from family members or others. Talk about the problem freely. In this way you will gain understanding, support and advice.
- *Do not* pay any outstanding debts that the gambler may have. Again, this just makes it easy for the gambler to shirk responsibility and avoid confronting and dealing with problems that he/ she has generated. Ask yourself: why should someone give up gambling if other people pay

their debts? This can of course be difficult, especially if you are a parent dealing with a gambler son or daughter. It is hard to see them suffer, risk legal action and/or jeopardise their future credit ratings. However, a balance must be achieved between these types of problem and the longer-term consequences of continued excessive gambling. The aim of all this is to teach the gambler to be responsible for any problems caused by gambling and that it is up to him/her and not others to fix any damage.

- Do not treat or regard the gambler as someone who is suffering a disease over which he/she has no control. Some gamblers use the ploy of arguing that they failed in their efforts to stop gambling simply because they were ill. Blaming an illness for their behaviour is totally unacceptable. Pathological gambling is not an illness defined by an *inability* to control behaviour but is rather a *failure* to control behaviour. Gamblers fail to control themselves rather than being unable to do so.

Review of Step 1

Understanding the true reasons why you are attempting to overcome your problem gambling is essential for success.

Only by being motivated for the right reasons will you continue to push yourself during periods of difficulty and remain faithful to the programme. Ask yourself the following questions:

- Are you doing this for your own benefit?
- Have you written down the benefits for your family and yourself of overcoming problem gambling?
- Are you realistic in pursuing the goal of controlled gambling?
- What alternative steps have you considered if experience shows you are not capable of handling controlled gambling?

Having determined your level of motivation, in Step 2 we can proceed to track and examine more closely the actual level of your gambling activity.

Step 2

Monitoring your gambling

It is all too easy to convince yourself that you do not spend too much money gambling. Research has shown that most people tend to remember wins easily and to forget losses quickly. This bias in memory leads to the false perception that you are winning more than you lose. How often have you boasted that you won, say, fifty pounds, conveniently ignoring the fact that you spent and lost seventy pounds trying to win that amount? Most gamblers think in the short term: how much they won or lost in today's session, or in the last week. This time period is too short as wins are possible after one session of gambling but, as you know from your very own experience, the longer you gamble, the more you are guaranteed to lose. So, when monitoring your gambling behaviour, you need to take a longer-term perspective. How much are you ahead or behind over the last six to twelve months? This will give you a more realistic guide as to how you are going with gambling.

There are a number of reasons why monitoring your gambling is a useful strategy in overcoming it.

- Keeping a record of your activities will force you to become aware of exactly how much money you are actually gambling.
- You will be able to keep track of changes in your level of gambling as you follow the instructions in this book. Your motivation will increase greatly once you see improvement happening.
- Detailed records will reveal particular patterns in your gambling, for example, regularly gambling after work, in response to stress or when you are depressed. Knowing the pattern of your habit will allow you to reorganise your schedule or take alternative strategies to deal with high-risk situations.

Monitoring requires effort and consistency. At times it may feel tedious and too bothersome, and is often avoided with the excuse that there was no paper or pen handy. However, do not underestimate the importance of monitoring, particularly as a useful means of picking up possible slips early on and so preventing them from developing into a relapse. If you are going to succeed, you must know how you are progressing over time. Once monitoring becomes a routine part of your practice, you will find it an invaluable tool for motivating you to keep up your efforts. It will also lead you to fully understand how much you have gambled and how it is affecting your quality of life.

A structured guide for monitoring

The key here is to record your gambling activity each day on a standard monitoring sheet. This section sets out a good example of such a sheet and offers guidelines on how best to record useful information on it.

Before we examine the recording process in detail, it is worth noting a few points that will make it easier for you to monitor your behaviour.

- Prepare enough standard monitoring sheets for daily use. You could use a tablet or smartphone to download an app that will enable you to record daily transactions.
- Use a separate sheet for each day.
- Make sure that you do not forget to take your daily monitoring sheet, tablet or smartphone when you leave home.
- Keep all the completed sheets or records together in one folder or app.
- Record your gambling transactions immediately; do not rely on memory at the end of the day.

> • You will need to record not only the actual transactions, but also your thoughts and feelings before each gambling session, and after learning the result of each bet. This will make it easier for you to identify patterns in your behaviour.

A good example of a completed monitoring sheet is provided in Figure 1. (Blank sheets for your use are provided at the end of the book. You can copy these into your tablet or smartphone.) You can use this monitoring sheet for any form of betting, of course; substitute your own form of gambling, for example, casino games, electronic gaming machines or cards, where appropriate. Monitor each form of gambling that you engage in, as this will give you an excellent idea as to which form of gambling is causing the most losses, and the total amount that you are losing over time. This will also help you to avoid thinking that because you are winning on one form of gambling, you are doing the same on all forms and are ahead overall.

In column 1, simply record the time and the specific place where you gambled. This will be helpful, as we shall see shortly, in making a list of high-risk situations to avoid.

In column 2, describe in detail all thoughts you may have had leading to your decision to gamble. This task is not as easy as it sounds and requires a lot of practice. Spend time trying to be as precise as possible and do not be satisfied with general statements. For example, you may be feeling upset.

Think of what has upset you: was it a critical remark made by your boss, did you have an argument with your wife, are you worried about some outstanding bills to pay? Did you think gambling would help you forget about your worries, discharge some of your anger and tension, or were you desperate to get the money and convinced that this was the only way to get it quickly and easily? What was the effect of these thoughts on your feelings? Were you depressed, highly anxious and agitated, worried sick or a combination of all of these emotions? It is sufficient to make notes in point form rather than sentences if you wish, but it is important to capture the very essence of your thoughts and feelings.

Now take a few moments to rate your level of tension. Use a ten-point scale where a rating of 1 represents no tension present and a rating of 10 indicates very high tension or anxiety. You do not have to limit yourself to rating tension. If you wish, you can substitute depression for tension. Or better still, add another rating scale to cover emotions such as anger, hopelessness and low self-esteem.

The next column, column 3, is reserved for recording any money borrowed to gamble, irrespective of its source. State the amount borrowed and from whom, and keep a running total of how much you owe that person or financial institution altogether. It's not pleasant to be reminded of your debts, but confronting them will make you realise just how much debt you are building up. A loan of twenty pounds may not seem much until you recall the fact that you already owe a substantial amount to that person; this may cause you to think twice.

FIGURE 1

Date: .... Day: ....

1	2	3	4	5	6	7	8
Time and place	Feelings and thoughts before gambling (rating of tension on ten-point scale – 1 = low, 10 = high)	Borrowings	Cash at start of session	Cash at end of session	Win	Loss	Feelings associated with results (rating of tension on ten-point scale – 1 = low, 10 = high)
1.20 p.m. Betting venue near work.	Stressful day, worried about bills to pay. Can I win some money? (7)		45	10		35	Angry, more depressed. Worried where I will get more money from. (8)
2.20 p.m. Betting venue near work.	Form guide. Saw favourite horse at good odds. (1)		10	85	75		Happy, I'm on a roll. Another win will see me out of trouble. (1)
4.30 p.m. Betting venue near home.	Talked to a friend. Given tip for horse or suggestions to socialise in venue. Confident that I can win enough now to pay off all outstanding debts. The chance I have been waiting for. Borrow 20 pounds. (1)	20 From David, work mate. Now owe him 50 in total (but will be able to repay after winning).	75	0		95	Depressed. Angry at myself for losing money I couldn't afford. (10)
Total wins/losses and borrowings		20			75	130	Loss: 75 - 130 = -55 Borrowing: = 20

A word of caution. Many people panic because of their debt and believe that their only chance of reducing it is by further gambling. When they become aware of the full extent of their debt, judgment is clouded by anxiety, heightening the urge to gamble. Remember: *gambling led you into debt; gambling will NOT lead you out of it*.

At the conclusion of each sheet's recordings, add the total for this column to see how much borrowed money you are prepared to risk.

Column 4 is designed to keep track of the amount of your own money spent on gambling. Record only the cash in hand, excluding borrowings. Money withdrawn from savings accounts or redirected from other purposes such as rent or bills should be listed in the 'Borrowings' column. We are interested only in the disposable or 'spare' cash physically in your possession. Winnings from previous bets or earlier sessions can be included. This information is useful for fully appreciating the amount turned over by you in a period of time – money that could be more productively spent. In the sample in Figure 1, the turnover is 45+10+75=130.

For column 5, record the cash remaining, if any, at the conclusion of the gambling session.

The whole purpose of gambling, some think, is to win money. Columns 6 and 7, recording winnings and losses on each bet, will help quickly to dispel this myth. Simply subtract the total in column 7 from that in column 6 (in the sample, 75-130=-55). The difference between these two figures gives your position at the end of the day. If the figure is a negative one, it means you have lost. I suspect that you will find that, more often than not, the figure will be negative.

Finally, in column 8, you need to record your thoughts and feelings at the end of the session. As before, rate your emotions on the ten-point scale. In the example, you are rating tension, but again you are free to change this to depression or any other feeling you wish to monitor. Remember, it is helpful to write down more than just a description, say, for example, 'depressed'. Specify *why* you are depressed, for example: 'I have let myself down again, I'm just a hopeless case.'

You will need to keep details of the final figure from your calculation of columns 6 and 7 on each sheet as a record of your progress. To do this you will need to use a separate sheet to record wins and losses from each daily completed monitoring sheet. For example, let us say that the sheet in Figure 1 records the first day's gambling in a particular week. We are interested in seeing how much you won or lost at the end of the week by keeping a running summary of your daily activities over a seven-day period, as shown in Table 2, opposite.

You won 103 pounds but also lost 208 pounds, giving you an overall loss for that week of 105 pounds.

Running total of wins and losses

TABLE 2		
Date: .... Week:		
Date	**Wins**	**Losses**
Day 1		55
Day 2	24	
Day 3		56
Day 4	67	
Day 5		23
Day 6	12	
Day 7		74
Total	103	208

Reviewing your progress

Once you have completed monitoring your gambling activity over a week, you should review your progress in detail. This exercise will enable you to chart changes over time and will provide valuable information for you to work out what triggers your urges and causes you to lose control. Reviewing your comments about your emotions and the ratings given for each day will allow you to see any patterns in your behaviour. Once you have established the links between external stresses, your thoughts and emotions and attitudes toward gambling, and application of the techniques to be described in this book, you will be well on the way to overcoming problem gambling.

Here are some useful questions to ask when you come to study your monitoring sheets:

* Are there particular times when I am most likely to gamble?
* Are there specific stresses or emotions that trigger my urge at these times?
* Does the urge start after I have discussed gambling topics with friends or heard reference to gambling on the television or radio?
* Is there a regular venue I go to gamble and feel comfortable?
* Is there a consistent pattern of emotions associated with winning?
* What about losing? What are my most likely reactions after a loss?
* Does the rate of gambling increase when I am upset? Do I binge when down?

Let us review our example above. In column 2, it is clear that the trigger for gambling is worry associated with not having money to pay bills. Your level of tension is already high, but increases after losing. Tension drops dramatically when you are confident of winning and have won, and continues to be low as your confidence is raised again. But after you have lost at the end of the day's gambling, your tension is rated at the maximum, and you are also depressed.

Now that you are aware of this pattern, you can take steps to dampen your unrealistic enthusiasm when you are given a tip or following a win. Write down on a small index card the following phrase:

Even though I am happy and confident now, how will I feel WHEN I LOSE?

Place this card in your wallet or purse where you hide your gambling money. Read it every time you have the urge to gamble. Basically, you know that eventually you *will lose* gambling. You have proved this to yourself ever since you started gambling; otherwise you would not be where you are today.

The practical advantage of understanding the emotions and situations that trigger your gambling is that you will be ideally placed to apply the cognitive behavioural techniques outlined in the following steps. Therefore, you must not cut corners when you monitor. Resist the temptation to think that you know your own habits; many people are surprised to find out the difference between what they think they do and what they actually do in real life.

I cannot stress enough how important it is to keep accurate records. You should allocate a fixed time each week, when you are not rushed and have plenty of time, to go over the monitoring sheets. It is very helpful to talk to your supporting partner or health professional about what you have written. They should be able to pick up on things that you may have perhaps overlooked or give you suggestions to think about.

Monitoring sheets for your use

Blank copies of the daily monitoring sheet and weekly summary sheet are provided below for your use. First, make a number of photocopies of the sheets or copy them into your tablet or smartphone for use over the coming weeks (some spare sheets are already provided at the end of the book). Then fill a couple in as samples, using the guidelines in the text above, to familiarise yourself with the process.

Daily monitoring sheet

Date: .... Day: ....

1	2	3	4	5	6	7	8
Time and place	Feelings and thoughts before gambling (rating of tension on ten-point scale – 1 = low, 10 = high)	Borrowings	Cash at start of session	Cash at end of session	Win	Loss	Feelings associated with results (rating of tension on ten-point scale – 1 = low, 10 = high)
Total wins/losses and borrowings							

Running summary of weekly activities

Date: .... Week: ....

Date	Wins	Losses
Day 1		
Day 2		
Day 3		
Day 4		
Day 5		
Day 6		
Day 7		
Total		

Review of Step 2

Have you made enough copies of the monitoring sheets to use over the next few weeks? It is a good idea to overestimate the number of copies needed; it is best to have spares rather than to risk running short.

Now, before moving on to the next step, make sure you are familiar with the process. Are you writing down enough information about your mood and stresses, so that when you study it you will be able to see any patterns that are present? Noting what thoughts frequently enter your mind when you have the urge to gamble will help you later on when you try to identify the irrational thoughts and ideas about gambling that act as a fertiliser to feed your problem gambling habits. Are you recording details immediately, when they happen, or relying on memory by writing things down at the end of the day? With problem gambling, memory is often not only inaccurate, but also biased in the way it selectively remembers certain information. There is a tendency to underestimate amounts lost and to minimise unpleasant emotions. Preferring to recall wins and positive feelings is a self-defeating strategy merely designed to justify more gambling.

Are you reviewing the monitoring sheets regularly? Do not simply glance at them, but study the relationship between various aspects of what you have recorded.

Finally, remember that it is in your own interest to be honest in your responses. Honesty reflects an attitude of commitment to help yourself. This is the very foundation of self-help.

Step 3

Controlling your urge using a relaxation technique

Even though I have the greatest intention in the world to stop gambling, once I have the urge, nothing else matters. I just don't think of the consequences, of what might happen if I lose. Everything apart from the gambling is blocked out of my mind; I'm so confident that I will win. If something gets in my way and prevents me from gambling, I get frustrated and irritable. I can only think of ways in which I may be able to satisfy my urge as quickly as possible.

Albert

It is common to hear the complaint that the urge to gamble is overwhelming and beyond control. As you have no doubt learnt from your monitoring, no matter what the cause, the drive to gamble follows a similar pattern. First comes the trigger. This might be stress at work or home, others talking of their own gambling or references to gambling in the media. Inability to handle work or family pressures or general dissatisfaction with your life may cause you to think about gambling as a release of tension or way of escaping. Once the thought enters your mind, it becomes difficult to shake off. Fantasies of a major win and what it would do to your lifestyle enter your mind. The pressure to find money to pay your bills fuels the urge when your belief is that your luck must change and that you are confident that a win is about to happen. A win may have saved you just in time to pay a debt on one occasion and you 'know' that this can happen again. You begin to feel confident of coming out ahead, and at the same time fearful that you may miss out on this opportunity. The last thing that you would want is to not have a bet only to see someone else win instead of you. This regret of not having taken action and missing out is very painful. The confidence and the urge grow with every passing moment. Concentration is impossible as your mind becomes absorbed with the task of gambling. Physical symptoms of tension such as restlessness, short temper and racing heart are obvious signs of anticipation and excitement. This tension continues to build until such time as the urge is finally satisfied through gambling.

What happens if you try to resist the urge? Any attempt to break the sequence by not gambling is met with a rising tide of anxiety and stress. The nagging doubt that, 'this time my luck has changed, I could win' plagues you. As one gambler said, 'I would just die if I missed out and my numbers came up, I can't afford to take the chance this time.' It is a catch-22 position: you'll feel bad if you gamble and bad if you don't.

Tackling the urge to gamble

In this section you will learn a simple but highly effective technique to reduce or eliminate the compelling urge that drives you to gamble. This technique is called 'imaginal desensitisation' and has been developed and described by an Australian psychiatrist, Professor Nathaniel McConaghy. Simply put, this technique involves learning a brief muscle-relaxation procedure and then imagining yourself about to gamble but walking away from the scene without doing so while applying the relaxation technique. Used consistently, imaginal desensitisation breaks the cycle between gambling and physical tension. It has been systematically evaluated by research and shown to be a valuable tool that you can easily apply to the particular setting relevant to you. Its strength lies in its ability to dampen down the tension associated with the urge to gamble, allowing you to use additional cognitive strategies that will be described in the next step.

Let us describe in more detail the late Professor McConaghy's model of the 'behaviour completion mechanism' as it applies to gambling. This will assist you in gaining a solid understanding of when and how to use the technique. The model is shown in diagram form in Figure 2.

We start off by coming into contact with opportunities to gamble. This may be through friends or family inviting us to have fun. It is clear that the more regularly and frequently a person gambles, the more established the habit becomes. The stronger the habit, the lower is the threshold triggering the urge. It does not take much to elicit a response from someone who gambles daily as compared to a person who gambles merely once a year.

Certain changes take place in the functioning of the brain once a habit is established. Without going into too much detail about these changes, it can be said that a mental model of the repeated habit is formed in our minds. This mental representation consists of all the links in a chain of behaviours that go to make up the total habit. For example, if we wish to pick up a glass and have a drink, a mental model of reaching out for a glass of water is activated in our mind. We start by moving our hand toward the glass. If our hand misses the glass, our intended action has not been completed. This causes a mild state of tension, which motivates us to adjust our behaviour so that it is completed satisfactorily.

In this model, once the first link in a chain of behaviours that form a habit is activated, the whole mental model becomes activated and motivates or drives us to complete the behaviour. This motivation or drive is referred to as the 'behaviour completion mechanism'.

Many gamblers are aware that their compulsion arises in response to a wide range of gambling-related cues, for example, reading the form guide, lottery results or walking past electronic gaming machines or off-track betting offices. Though you may find it hard to believe, it is crucial to note that the compulsion is also frequently triggered by factors that do not appear to have any direct relationship with gambling, such as boredom, time of day, or apparently unrelated stresses. For example, an office worker may find

Figure 2 Behaviour completion mechanism

his thoughts turning to gambling just before lunch-time when he often goes to the pub or bookmakers to play gaming machines. A housewife home alone all day may find herself anxiously waiting for everyone to leave for work or school so she can go out to play bingo; no such urge to gamble is felt on weekends when she knows everyone will be home. Typically, the urge to gamble manifests itself in response to situations of tension or stress.

Through repeated episodes we come to recognise that gambling is exciting and allows us to escape negative mood states of anxiety and depression. It is enjoyable. But gambling also results in losses that aggravate our financial stress, causing further depression and anxiety. These emotions then feed back and themselves become cues to trigger the neuronal 'behaviour completion' model, which precipitates the urge to return to gambling. As indicated in Figure 2, cognitive therapy can be used to short-circuit this pathway by providing a way to challenge distorted beliefs and teaching alternative stress management and problem-solving skills to prevent negative emotions from turning into gambling cues.

What happens if there is an attempt to prevent the habit from being carried out to completion? The neuronal model remains incomplete and a sense of unpleasant physical tension is produced. This tension persists until one finally acts out the habit completely. The reduction in tension following completion of the habit reinforces the cycle.

Imaginal desensitisation works by preventing this build-up in tension and therefore its release in repeated gambling. The rehearsing of familiar gambling behaviour patterns 'in imagination' while in a physically relaxed state ensures that uncontrollable levels of tension are no longer provoked by relevant cues. In this manner, the rise in tension associated with the habit not being completed is short-circuited. The drive to carry out the habit is diminished, making it easier to control the urge.

The primary purpose of imaginal desensitisation is to reduce:

> - the urge to gamble;
> - the excitement associated with gambling;
> - the persistent tension produced by attempts to resist the urge.

The benefit of imaginal desensitisation is that, once you have mastered it, it enables you to apply an easily learnt technique in the real-life situation as soon as the urge starts to develop.

Learning imaginal desensitisation

Imaginal desensitisation is a simple relaxation-based technique that combines physical relaxation with mental images of being confronted with an opportunity to gamble but not doing so. The instructions for the relaxation procedure and guided mental images will be recorded on a recording device for use in each self-help session. The following summary will help you to understand the number of steps involved and how they fit together, before we move on to the actual construction of the recording.

You will need a paper and pen or pencil to write down a set of descriptions, and a recording device with a thirty-minute capacity to record instructions for later use. (While it is possible for a partner or friend to read out the instructions during each session, it is usually more efficient and convenient to record these. This allows you to complete a session on your own whenever you have time.)

To prepare the recording:

- Write down a description of a typical example of your pattern of gambling.
- Follow the guidelines given in the section below on how to break down your description into a series of smaller steps or scenes, and how and where to include the relaxation instructions.
- Following this pattern, read out aloud and record on your recording device a description of your gambling habit, together with instructions on how to relax your muscles.
- The recorded session is now ready for use.

Each audio file recorded in this way will contain a set of instructions guiding you through a series of gambling scenes while you maintain a state of physical relaxation, passing through the following stages:

- Relaxation instructions.
- Instructions guiding you to imagine the first scene of your gambling habit.
- Relaxation instructions.
- Instructions guiding you to imagine the second scene of your gambling habit.
- Relaxation instructions.
- Instructions guiding you to imagine the third scene of your gambling habit.
- Relaxation instructions.
- Instructions guiding you to imagine the fourth scene of your gambling habit.
- Relaxation instructions.

There may be more than four scenes; four to six is usually an appropriate number.

Each recorded imaginal desensitisation will need to be played two to three times for the first five days and then once a day until you have fully learnt the skill. After that, you may use the recording as needed.

Now let us move on to the first step in constructing the imaginal desensitisation audio recordings.

Constructing a series of gambling scenes

This technique requires you to provide a description of your typical gambling habits, and then to think beyond them. Recall the last three or four occasions when you gambled. Take a few moments to write down the sequence of events that took place on each occasion, from when you first had the urge until you actually gambled. Add to this a description of your feelings when you have lost. Now add how you would feel if you were able to anticipate these feelings *before* you gambled, and use them to deter you from gambling. In recording the sequence, describe each scene as though it were one link in a chain. Let me guide you with an example of a sequence written down by a casino gambler.

Scene 1: I am at work feeling upset because my boss criticised me. My thoughts turn to the casino and unwinding by having a drink and spending time playing roulette and the gaming machines. I am sure that my luck will change and I will win. Although I am working, I keep thinking of visiting the nearby casino immediately after work. I am looking at the time, a sense of urgency to finish work so I can start playing.

Scene 2: Heading toward the casino. In the near distance I can see the sign and other patrons entering. Approaching, walking closer and closer. Thoughts of winning this time enter my mind. A sense of confidence. I will beat the system and win at roulette and the machines this time.

Scene 3: Entering the casino. I can hear the sounds of the gaming machines and players at the table talking and yelling with excitement. Other patrons are looking at the table games. One or two people are at the cashiers cashing in their winnings. The atmosphere is electric. I can hardly wait to start playing.

Scene 4: I walk over to the roulette table. I look at the wheel spinning and anticipate the number that the ball will stop at. I start to work out how many chips I should place on my chosen number. I feel confident this time of picking a winner.

Scene 5: As I stand there about to place the chips on the table, I look around at the other people standing around. I begin to think of after the wheel stops, how I will feel when I lose. I remember the feeling of despair when my number fails to come up. Angry, I feel like kicking myself for thinking that I really could win. I usually think of what else I could have done with the cash instead of wasting it. I take a close look at the others in the casino. Some look happy but most look like they have lost.

Scene 6: Bored. Even if I do win this time, I know that I will give it back eventually through my losses. Bored with the idea of standing there picking numbers I hope will come up, I turn around and start walking out of the casino. I am in control of my urge. Giving up this opportunity to gamble and deciding to return home makes me feel good.

Write down in the blank forms provided three or four such sequences, making sure that you have in each at least three or four scenes describing your typical behaviour approaching your favourite form of gambling, followed by two or three scenes of you thinking about the unpleasant emotions following a loss and of being bored with the idea of gambling.

SEQUENCE 1
Scene 1:   ....
Scene 2:   ....
Scene 3:   ....
Scene 4:   ....
Scene 5:   ....
Scene 6:   ....

SEQUENCE 2
Scene 1:   ....
Scene 2:   ....
Scene 3:   ....
Scene 4:   ....
Scene 5:   ....
Scene 6:   ....

SEQUENCE 3

Scene 1:

....

....

Scene 2:

....

....

Scene 3:

....

....

Scene 4:

....

....

Scene 5:

....

....

Scene 6:

....

....

SEQUENCE 4

Scene 1:

....

....

Scene 2:

....

....

Scene 3:

....

....

Scene 4:

....

....

Scene 5:

....

....

Scene 6:

....

....

Relaxation techniques

Having developed a series of typical patterns of behaviour, we now need to learn a brief muscle-relaxation technique. There are a number of different approaches to relaxing. The self-help book on *Overcoming Panic* in this series is a good reference and contains detailed instructions on the various relaxation techniques that are available. If you like, you may wish to purchase a commercially available relaxation download or CD.

The relaxation technique that we will be using here is a brief version of a progressive muscle-relaxation procedure that is widely used for the management of stress and anxiety. Certain muscle groups such as those in the hands, arms, stomach and legs are systematically tensed for a few moments; then the tension is gradually released, allowing a sense of relaxation to flow through these parts of the body. To practise this technique, it is best to find a quiet time and place where you will be free from distractions and interruptions for about half an hour. Choose a comfortable couch or chair in which you can sit quietly with your eyes closed while you follow the instructions given to you on the recording.

With this 'mini version' of muscle relaxation, you will be able to train yourself to relax effectively in almost any situation where you find the gambling urge emerging.

A practice session of imaginal desensitisation

The imaginal desensitisation process involves imagining the gambling scenes you have recorded while at the same time applying the relaxation procedure. Each session should include three or four sequences, and each sequence should take five minutes to complete. This means that, including the relaxation instructions, one whole session will be about twenty minutes in length.

Let us begin with a step-by-step example of a treatment session.

Preparation

- Find a quiet comfortable space where you will not be disturbed for half an hour. Sit in a relaxing chair; or you may prefer to lie down on a couch.
- Close your eyes, settle down and focus your attention on your breathing. Take a breath, hold it, and now slowly let it out saying the word 'relax'. Let go of all the tension in the muscles in your body with each slow breath out.
- Concentrate on the instructions as they are read out or played on the recording. It is important that you keep a focus on imagining the scenes being presented. Do not allow yourself to drift off or become distracted by, for example, thinking of tasks you have to do.
- Most importantly, do not drift off into sleep. This is an active technique that requires effort and attention on your part. Relaxation is not simply

becoming drowsy or dozing. Proper relaxation will reduce your muscle tension, slowing down your rate of breathing and metabolism while you are still awake.

- How vividly you are able to visualise scenes is not important. Good results have been achieved with people who are poor at mental imagery. The key to success is combining the relaxation with (even weak) images of gambling.

Instructions to be recorded on your recording device

We are now ready to commence recording a session for use. Let us start the procedure using one sequence as an example to follow.

The following instructions are to be read out aloud and audio-recorded:

Make yourself comfortable on the chair. Close your eyes and clear your mind of any thoughts or images and focus your attention on your breathing . . . [pause] . . . Take a deep breath and let it out slowly . . . [pause] . . . Just breathing easily and gently now, no effort, breathing as you normally would. Now, as you breathe out I want you to say to yourself, 'Relax'.

Now I want you to clench your hands into fists as tightly as you can. Focus your mind on the tension building up in your hands and the rest of your body . . . [pause] . . . Hold that tension there . . . [pause] . . . notice how uncomfortable that tension feels . . . [pause] . . . holding it for a moment longer . . . [pause] . . . Now relax, let go of the muscles and allow your hands to relax, relax your hands and your arms. Allow the tension to flow out . . . [pause] . . . allow the tension to flow down your arms and out of your fingers. Clearing your mind of thoughts, focusing your attention on your hands and your arms . . . [pause] . . . allowing your hands and arms to become heavier and heavier, letting yourself become more and more relaxed, repeating the word 'relax' as you breathe out . . . [pause] . . . allowing your hands and arms to become heavier and heavier.

Now, turning your attention to your neck and shoulders, let that feeling of relaxation in your hands and your arms move up to your neck and shoulders . . . [pause] . . . letting your head fall forward as it begins to feel relaxed . . . [pause] . . . letting your shoulders go . . . [pause] . . . just feel the tension flowing down your arms out of your hands and fingers, down your body and out of your legs and feet as you are relaxing your whole body . . . [pause] . . . just continue relaxing, noticing how nice and peaceful you are beginning to feel, just letting all of the tension out . . . [pause] . . . feel it flowing down your neck and shoulders, through your arms and out of your hands and fingers, down your body into your legs and out of your feet . . . [pause] . . . your whole body becoming heavier and heavier, more and more relaxed . . . [pause] . . . slowing your thoughts down and focusing your attention on your body, allowing yourself to become heavier and heavier, becoming very relaxed . . . [pause] . . . Just continue relaxing for a while longer.

SEQUENCE 1

Scene 1: Now imagine that you are at work. It's been a bad day; your boss has criticised you over something you've done. You feel resentful and tense and want to get away from it all. As you brood over your problems, thoughts of the casino come to mind. You think of how playing roulette and the machine at the casino helps you to unwind and relax, and particularly the excitement that you feel when winning. You realise that it's not long to finishing time now. Your thoughts turn to heading off toward the casino straight after work . . . You feel a strong urge to go to the casino, you have been thinking about it for several hours. You can hardly wait until work finishes . . . [pause] . . . Looking forward to the excitement of playing roulette and the machines. Recall how you felt in the past as you think about going to the casino straight after work. But as you do so, let yourself become relaxed, let the tension out of your body . . . [pause] . . . Allow yourself to become more and more relaxed with each breath out, feel the tension flow out of your body.

Recall the thoughts in your mind as you think about going to the casino, looking forward to backing your favourite numbers and playing your favourite machine, confident that you can win, a strong expectation that you will win this time. You feel good: thinking of playing helps you forget work problems. Also, you remember that you need to pay some bills. There is a lot of pressure on you to get some money to pay those debts. Let yourself relax as your mind focuses on this scene, feeling your muscles becoming even more relaxed, loose and floppy as you visualise this scene . . . [pause] . . . Continue relaxing . . .

You've got nothing else planned after work, you want to give yourself some time out and unwind. Recall the excitement of gambling . . . [pause] . . .

Continue to focus on letting yourself relax . . . [pause] . . .

Scene 2: You're now heading for the casino. You're getting closer and closer. You can see the casino in the distance, the large neon sign flashing the casino's name, the people walking in and out. Recall the feelings as you near the entrance, the anticipation, and the strong urge to go in and place some bets. Try to recall those feelings . . . [pause] . . . You're confident that you will win this time, luck's on your side . . . [pause] . . . Now is the chance that you have been waiting for.

But as you keep recalling those feelings, I want you to keep focusing on relaxing. Allow yourself to continue to relax, saying in your mind the word 'relax' as you breathe out, feeling all of the tension flowing away, out through your hands and your feet . . . [pause] . . .

Scene 3: Imagine yourself entering the casino, going in through the lobby. Now imagine yourself inside. Try to recall the excitement . . . [pause] . . . The noise of machines playing, the rows of tables, the television channels showing races and sports events on large screens in the sports pit. The excitement is in the atmosphere. People milling around playing table games and the machines. You can hear them talking about the cards and numbers that have come their way. Try to visualise this scene as clearly as you can . . . [pause] . . . Try to recall the emotions and feelings you have experienced, recall the anticipation. Allow yourself to relax as much as you can while you visualise this scene, letting all the tension flow away . . . [pause] . . .

Scene 4: Imagine yourself as you walk over to a roulette table. You look at the recent numbers that have come up shown on the board next to the croupier. Start to think of the money that you need as you are standing there looking at the numbers that you feel will come up on the next spin of the wheel. Feeling the anticipation rising in your body as you are standing there trying to pick which number is most likely to come up . . . [pause] . . . Allowing yourself to relax, focusing on your breathing, as you are concentrating on the scene in your head . . . [pause] . . .

You are watching others placing their chips all over the table, the croupier moving to pick up the ball . . . [pause] . . . confident that your number is a sure thing to come up next, you start to think of placing your chips down on the table . . . as you see yourself standing there, allow yourself to relax, focusing on your breathing . . . [pause] . . . Let yourself become physically more and more relaxed as you visualise the scene . . . [pause] . . .

Scene 5: As you are standing there, your thoughts turn to previous occasions, of the times when you lost and the feelings associated with losing . . . [pause] . . . You realise that you are probably not going to win this time either. You start to think of how you feel when you lose, when you are left short of money at the end of the day . . . [pause] . . . The bills that still need to be paid. You're starting to have second thoughts about spending your time and money in the casino. Thinking about the time you are wasting and the money you will be losing. You begin to get bored. You start looking at the people around you and you see just how bored they really look . . . [pause] . . . You think of playing the machines instead but looking at the players they too seem bored.

Let yourself recall these thoughts now, of how disappointed you were, the feelings of remorse for having spent time and money in the casino losing at roulette and the machines. Let yourself recall these feelings now. You are finding yourself becoming increasingly bored with spending time in the casino, with gambling . . . [pause] . . . You start to think of other things that you could be doing, of other things you could be spending your money on. Let yourself visualise this scene in your mind . . . [pause] . . . the feelings of boredom associated with gambling . . .

As you do this, continue to let yourself relax . . . [pause] . . . Let all of the tension flow out of your muscles . . . [pause] . . .

Scene 6: As you stand there at the table you think more and more of the times when you've made the wrong choice in the past and lost. You think of all the money you've lost. You recall how miserable you felt then . . . [pause] . . . You decide not to place your chips down. Instead, you ask the croupier to cash these in and turn away.

As you turn away let yourself relax, letting all of the tension flow away . . . [pause] . . . You're feeling heavier and heavier as your muscles go loose and floppy.

Now imagine yourself as you decide to walk out of the casino, deciding not to gamble, feeling relaxed and at ease with yourself . . . [pause] . . . You've decided to pass up this opportunity to gamble, feeling quite relaxed as you walk out. You still have your money . . . You leave the noise of the casino and walk outside, thinking of other things you could be doing with your time. You feel relaxed and in control, pleased with yourself and your decision . . . [pause] . . . quite content and relaxed having walked out of the casino, feeling good that you have decided not to gamble, happy with yourself . . . [pause] . . .

As you do this, let yourself continue to relax, letting all of the tension flow away, feeling heavier and heavier as your muscles go loose and floppy . . . [pause] . . .

Giving up this opportunity to gamble, deciding to go home, feeling quite good, feeling in control of your urges,

feeling satisfied with the decision you have made . . . [pause]
. . .

Keep visualising this scene as you allow yourself to continue to relax as much as you can.

Closing instructions for Sequence 1: Now clear your mind of all thoughts and allow yourself to relax . . . [pause] . . . Put all other thoughts out of your mind and focus attention back on to your body, letting yourself relax . . . [pause] . . . becoming more and more relaxed, sinking down into the chair. Just continue relaxing now for a few minutes . . . [pause] . . . Letting the tension flow out of your body, becoming more and more relaxed. Enjoy that feeling . . . [pause] . . . Keep relaxing and focusing your attention on your body. Let all other thoughts out of your mind.

Now follow the relaxation instructions given at the start of the session for the next two to three minutes.

Then continue with the next sequence. Repeat exactly the same set of instructions as above, but substitute the set of gambling-related scenes you wrote down for your second sequence. Then go through the process with each of the other sequences.

Remember, each of the sequences is made up of three or four gambling-related scenes followed by two or three scenes related to boredom and the unpleasant feelings you experience after a loss. Three or four sequences together make up a full session lasting about twenty minutes.

After you have completed the third or fourth sequence, read out the closing instructions for the session:

Closing instructions: Allow any tension to flow out of your body as you visualise this scene . . . [pause] . . . letting yourself become more and more relaxed as you do so. Continue relaxing as you let the tension out. Now, clear your mind of all your thoughts. Just focusing on your body . . . [pause] . . . letting all of the tension out and letting yourself become more and more relaxed, enjoying that peaceful sensation of relaxation . . . [pause] . . . Just continue relaxing now for a few minutes longer. When you decide to get up, open your eyes slowly, stretch your muscles and slowly rise.

You have now successfully completed the audio recording of the session.

Effects of imaginal desensitisation

What effects can you expect once you have mastered the technique? Do not expect immediate noticeable changes. The effect of this therapy will become obvious over time, often a week or two after you have completed ten to fifteen sessions. Then you will notice that the drive to gamble is absent or so weak that you can easily control it.

After I had finished ten sessions I didn't think the technique worked. There was no difference in how I felt. But a strange thing happened as time went on. I noticed that I wasn't rushing to go to the casino, and when I did, there was no feeling of excitement left. It really struck me one day after work. My usual routine was to drop into the casino for a drink and play on my way home. But on this day, I actually forgot to walk in and went straight past it. I was surprised because it was only when I reached my front door that I realised I had walked straight past the casino without one thought of going in. My self-confidence has risen because I feel more able to control my urge when I am exposed to gambling situations. I can best describe the change as now being bored with the idea of gambling.

Andrew

Recommended timetable and additional hints

To make it easier to learn and apply the technique, try the following suggestions:

- For each sequence, write down each scene immediately followed by the relaxation instructions, as we have done in the above example.
- Repeat this step for each of the sequences you are going to use.

- Audio-record each session on a recording device. Read out the instructions aloud, slowly, with a pause between the sentences in each scene. Do not rush; give yourself sufficient time to imagine the scene and to relax adequately.
- Each scene should take about five minutes to complete, so take your time.
- Wait two or three minutes before proceeding to the next scene and relax during this time.

Now you are ready to train yourself in the technique. Practice is crucial; the more you practise, the more skilled you will become in applying the technique efficiently. To gain maximum benefit you should do two to three thirty-minute sessions each day for five days: that is, a minimum of ten sessions over one week. Allow two to three hours between each session. This has been shown to be the most effective schedule. After this you may use the recording as a booster session whenever the need arises.

Once you are confident you have mastered the technique, you will be able to put it into practice automatically whenever you experience an urge coming on. Do not become complacent. Continually apply the technique whenever you have an urge, no matter how small it may seem. Complacency is likely to result in a return of the drive to gamble.

A number of sensible gamblers have recommended the use of a recording device with earphones when they are away from home as a very helpful strategy. This is a good idea and worth using.

Review of Step 3

The relaxation procedure described in this step is a highly effective way of controlling your urge to gamble. You must use it whenever you experience an urge to gamble, no matter how small that urge feels.

It is best to record the instructions and use the audio device each time you practise. Alternatively, have someone supervise each session by reading out instructions to you.

Are you falling asleep or becoming distracted during sessions? If so, practise when you are not tired or sleepy. Make a special effort to focus on the instructions given to you. The more effort you put into learning the technique, the greater will be your reward.

Once you have completed at least ten to fourteen sessions over a week using the audio recording, you should be so familiar with the technique that you can do it on your own. Ideally, with practice you will be able to relax and apply the technique in less than three or four minutes. Then you can practise when you are travelling to work and in your lunch break. All you require is a few minutes of uninterrupted time.

Most importantly, are you learning to relax and visualise the scenes in real situations where you are exposed to gambling-related cues? This is a practical skill that you must put into effect when you are confronted with any cue that triggers your gambling urge.

Step 4

Controlling gambling-related cues

In Step 3, you learnt a relaxation procedure to use whenever an urge to gamble appeared at any stage. It should come as no surprise that a wide variety of cues associated with gambling, such as hearing friends talking about a hot favourite at the track, watching the lottery draw on television or walking past a betting office, can act as a trigger to set off that urge. In this day and age, pop-up advertisements on the Internet draw attention to casino games; television broadcasts of sporting events include visuals of online sports betting companies littered around the grounds; gambling industry sponsorship logos are plastered over sports uniforms; commentators offer odds; and social media-type games that mimic gambling games all serve to promote gambling. Gambling is now part and parcel of normal sporting and recreational activities. How and why do these cues come to trigger urges to gamble? Well, anticipation of winning money creates a sense of pleasure or excitement, that is, a positive feeling of physical arousal. This feeling is so strong at times that some gamblers describe it as being similar to a drug 'high'. Any cue or behaviour that occurs immediately beforehand is also likely to become associated with the excitement. This is called conditioning. These cues quickly become a signal activating gambling-related thoughts and feelings. Cues associated with gambling are now hard to avoid.

Physical environments as a trigger for gambling

You may be surprised to learn that in addition to cues directly related to gambling, places, times and even emotions can also act as triggers. When you regularly visit the casino, pub/club during the lunch break, go to the betting office on Saturday afternoon or read the form guide over breakfast, a regular pattern develops. Your excitement in anticipation of gambling becomes associated with these specific times. Later on, these times themselves turn into signals reminding you of gambling. A good example is that of hunger. Many people eat meals at regular times. When you notice the time an hour or so before your usual mealtime, you feel hunger because you know that it is time to eat soon, even though your body is not really starved. On the other hand, if you are busy and distracted and lose your sense of time, you do not feel any hunger until you next notice the time or when your body is really starved of nutrition.

When reviewing your monitoring sheets, look for any link between physical settings and your urge to gamble. Common settings that may act as triggers are:

- reading the form guide in the newspaper;
- seeing an amusement arcade while walking down the street;
- watching a television broadcast of the lottery draw or sporting event;
- going out to lunch at the local that is near the amusement arcade, betting office or casino;
- buying the Saturday morning paper;
- discussing race results with friends over a drink;
- listening to race/lottery results on the radio;
- being on the way home after work;
- noticing a betting office/casino as you walk/ drive by.

These are called 'situational cues'.

Write down the common situational cues that lead you to increase your gambling urge.

1 ....

2 ....

3 ....

4 ....

5 ....

6 ....

7 ....

8 ....

9 ....

10 ....

Hints on handling situational cues

An effective way of controlling your urge is to avoid any situation or activity that serves to remind you of gambling. This is easier said than done; after all, there are reminders of gambling almost everywhere we go – in advertising, sports and other media reports on winners, local betting shops and outlets, and discussions among friends. Even your tablet or smartphone can be a reminder of gambling; online gambling is now readily accessible and available in your pocket or briefcase. While you may not realistically be able to avoid every cue, there are ways of minimising your exposure to them.

Try some of the following.

- Deliberately avoid reading the paper's sports section containing the race results. Ask your partner to remove these before you start reading.

Once you lose contact with the form, your interest will gradually diminish.

- Turn off the television or radio when results are being broadcast. Do not listen and, more importantly, do not play mental games of picking the results to see how you would have done had you placed a bet. This is definitely to be avoided as it serves only to fuel your interest.

- When friends invite you to play the slot machines during the lunch break, politely decline. Suggest some alternative activity, for example, having a chat at a coffee shop or window shopping. Do not go with the intention of only watching. All that will happen is that your urge to join in will rise, especially if you see someone win. An excuse frequently made is that you will lose friends if you don't join in. But ask yourself, what is more important to you, socialising with these people or overcoming your gambling? The choice is yours. If these friends are close to you, let them know of the difficulty you have controlling your gambling. Ask for their cooperation in helping you. If they are true friends, they will go out of their way to help by not talking about gambling in your presence or inviting you to come gambling with them. If they do not respond, then ask yourself, are these true friends that are worth keeping?

If gambling is the only bond holding you and these friends together, I would have serious reservations about the quality of the relationships.

- If you gamble regularly on the way home, take a different route or offer someone a lift home. Having someone else present will make you think twice because of the need to explain where you are going.

- Arrange alternative activities with your family or friends during high-risk times. For example, invite friends over at weekends or organise an outing with family at times when you would normally gamble. Often the urge to gamble fades once you realise that there is no possibility of gambling because of other commitments.

- As you come into contact with a cue that sets off thoughts of gambling in your mind, apply the relaxation technique you have learnt. Take a deep breath, hold it for a slow count to three, then let your breath out slowly, saying the word 'relax' as you do so. Start your muscle relaxation by clenching your fists and then relaxing your whole body as you slowly let the tension out. Begin the imagery with the scenes you have learnt.

- Bring to mind the four most negative consequences you can think of should you act on your urge, gamble and lose. Do not fantasise about winning; you know from experience that you will most likely lose – if not on this next occasion, then certainly over the next few times. Always ask yourself: 'How will I feel *when*, and not *if*, I lose?

- Use Internet blocking options to prevent you accessing gambling sites on your desktop, tablet or smartphone.
- Avoid playing simulated gambling games on social media free-to-play sites.

Emotions as a trigger for gambling

In the field of addiction, it is well known that negative mood states of depression, anxiety and anger play a major role in causing loss of control to occur. For many people, gambling is an opportunity to escape from everyday stresses and problems surrounding them. Often you hear the gamblers say: 'I just couldn't cope, I felt so unhappy. Playing the fruit machines [betting on the horses, going to bingo] lets me forget about life altogether.' This is similar to what happens in alcohol addiction. Drinking enables the drinker to temporarily reduce their level of tension. So, whenever there is stress, the alcoholic is likely to drink. The same is true of gambling.

In these circumstances, reinforcement of gambling behaviour occurs in two ways. The first is the lift in mood resulting from the excitement of anticipating a win. Winning makes you feel good, improves your self-esteem and puts you into a physical state of positive arousal. Secondly, the concentration and excitement distract you from your worries and cares. In this way, becoming totally absorbed in gambling reduces your tension by shifting your attention away from unpleasant thoughts.

A similar situation may apply with respect to anger. Following an argument, people often respond with prolonged anger, becoming uptight and brooding about things that were said to them. They feel resentful and frustrated at not being able to handle the situation or get their own way, or are devastated by criticism aimed at them. This is a most unpleasant emotional state. In many respects, anger is an emotion that can be used productively if channelled properly into overcoming the sources of frustration. But unfortunately, many people tend to bottle up their anger inside, instead of expressing it appropriately. The build-up in anger needs to be discharged, and gambling is one readily available channel. Ask yourself, does your urge to gamble arise immediately after an argument? Do you feel like 'taking it out' on gambling?

Look at your monitoring sheet as described in Step 2 above. Can you identify any consistent pattern linking your gambling with unpleasant mood states or anger? If so, you are now in a good position to learn alternative strategies to eliminate unpleasant negative moods. There are a number of excellent self-help books in this series aimed at overcoming depression, anxiety and low self-esteem. Consult these for useful hints on how to reduce negative moods, as well as for detailed instructions on effective problem-solving strategies, which we do not have space here to examine in detail. Do not forget, too, that your local doctor or counsellor can also direct you to individual or group skills training to assist you.

Some common emotions triggering urges to gamble are:

- feelings arising from an argument at home;
- feelings arising from being criticised at work by my employer;
- stress and anxiety caused by interpersonal or work-related difficulties;
- worry about debts and/or not having enough money to pay bills;
- anxiety about people finding out how much I do actually gamble;
- fear that someone will find out about the money I stole to gamble;
- feeling generally unhappy with my life;
- anger at my partner/spouse for not paying me enough attention;
- resentment that my partner is spending all their time with the children and ignoring me;
- resentment that my partner is never at home;
- feeling a need to win the affection of my friend/partner through buying them things;
- distress that friends my age have so much more than me – car, home, stereo, etc. – and wanting to 'catch up' with them quickly.

Write down the emotions that you have noticed trigger your urge to gamble.

1 ....

2 ....

3 ....

4 ....

5 ....

6 ....

7 ....

8 ....

9 ....

10 ....

Hints on handling emotions: Stress management

It is all too easy to blame loss of control on your emotions. Wendy, a 25-year-old married secretary, was upset that her husband of two years was staying at work late almost every night. She felt that he was not showing interest in her and was afraid that he would have an affair. Miserable and unhappy, she would play the slot machines when she knew he would be home late. As time went on, she became angry toward him. She felt she was teaching him a lesson by losing all their savings. Part of her low self-esteem grew out of the fact that she believed that she was no longer able to control her behaviour and was at the mercy of her emotions.

In therapy, we discussed the importance of communicating her unhappiness and anger to her husband more directly and openly. She quickly realised that her husband was not aware of her feelings, let alone of her gambling. Following some joint therapy sessions, she was able to express her feelings, resulting in a change in her husband's work pattern. Her urge to gamble declined rapidly. At this point she accepted responsibility for her emotions and understood how they influenced her behaviour.

Some comments on stress management skills are relevant here, because we know that stress is one element that commonly leads to impaired control over behaviour. When overall stress levels are high, you may be more likely to be affected by worries over your ability to handle matters. You may be more likely to make poor decisions, which aggravate the situation. For example, inability to cope with stressful situations or anxiety often leads people to use alcohol or illicit drugs or to become dependent on anti-anxiety medication. Similarly, escape into gambling is a strategy used by some to cope with stress. However, the financial problems caused by gambling only add further to the existing stresses, resulting in a reinforced desire to escape through more gambling. And so the cycle continues.

LIFESTYLE STRESS

POOR STRESS
MANAGEMENT SKILLS

STRESS DUE TO FINANCIAL
STRAIN CAUSED BY LOSSES

ESCAPE INTO GAMBLING

Figure 3 Stress–gambling cycle

All of us experience general symptoms of stress on occasions, for example when we are confronted with pressure at work, failure to measure up to expectations, the birth of a baby or problems trying to save money for holidays or important purchases. The list of potentially stressful events is limitless; situations that some people find distressing are not at all distressing to others, and vice versa.

It is important to remember that not all stress is harmful, and most of us function better with some stress in our lives. A little anxiety before we have to take a test or give a speech may actually improve our performance as we become more alert and focused on the task. Too much stress, however, can overwhelm us. When this happens we tend to pay a lot of attention to the uncomfortable symptoms of stress rather than the task we have to do and our performance may suffer.

There are two parts to a stress response, the physical and the psychological. Some people tend to respond with physical symptoms of distress such as headaches, gastrointestinal pains or general lack of energy, while others tend to worry excessively, suffer low self-worth, feel pressured or become irritable. Review your monitoring sheets and see which type of reaction is most common for yourself.

Physical symptoms of stress include:

- muscle tension and weakness;
- increased heart rate;
- increased rapidity of breathing;
- headaches;
- gastrointestinal pains – stomach cramps, nausea;
- agitation.

Psychological symptoms include:

- sadness, feelings of worthlessness;
- low self-confidence;
- poor concentration and memory;
- constantly feeling under pressure;
- anxiety;
- irritability and short temper;
- excessive worry.

Before we consider how best to deal with excessive stress, try to pinpoint some of the sources of stress in your own life and identify why they are so stressful, using the blank list provided.

Source of stress	What makes this stressful situation so difficult to handle?
1.	
2.	
3.	
4.	
5.	

In reducing your overall stress levels, it is often useful to distinguish between *external* and *internal* sources of stress. External stressors are those that occur in our environment and may be beyond our immediate control. For example, criticism at work by an irritable boss, the car breaking down in heavy traffic, getting burgled or moving house are all considered to be external stressors because these events may not be under your direct control. Internal stressors, on the other hand, are those that we create for ourselves through negative attitudes, distorted thinking, poor time management and weak problem-solving skills. They may include the feelings of needing the love and approval of everyone you meet, the inability to say 'no' for fear of rejection, or the tendency to accept too many demands on your time and energy. Internal stressors are the most common sources of stress, and yet they are also the most frequently ignored or overlooked.

It is not unusual for people to experience a combination of external and internal stressors that interact with one another. For example, imagine your family wants you to take them away during the school holidays and you realise that you have hardly any savings left (external stressor). What if there is no opportunity to earn extra cash or to borrow from friends or the bank (external stressor)? What would you do? Would you start blaming yourself for being incompetent (internal stressor), working yourself up into such a state that you start thinking of any way of getting that money? Or would you try to discuss the matter with your spouse or partner to try to find a solution? Can you think of other approaches to solving the problem that do not involve turning to gambling?

People differ in the ways they cope with stress. Some coping skills, such as simply avoiding stressful situations, may be more effective in the short term than in the long term. Avoiding stressful situations by immersing yourself in gambling is a poor coping strategy as any relief gained is temporary.

In overcoming general symptoms of stress, both your physical and your psychological health need to be addressed. Because the mind and the body are so closely linked, physical ill health can result in mental ill health, and vice versa. For example, if you do not get adequate sleep or have not been maintaining a healthy diet, you may start to feel irritable or anxious. Alternatively, if you become depressed you may lose your appetite, lose weight and become run down. Conversely, many people report that they feel happier and more energised when they improve their level of fitness by undertaking a regular exercise programme. Strategies to improve your physical and mental health will be discussed in the sections that follow.

Improving your physical health

The main components of a programme to improve your physical health include sleep, exercise, diet and physical relaxation. If you focus on improving each of these aspects of your physical health, you will probably notice significant improvement in your ability to handle stress.

SLEEP

Everyone has different requirements for the amount of sleep they need. In addition, some people function better late at night, while others may find that they are most alert in the mornings. By recognising what your normal sleep requirements are and when you are most alert, you may be able to modify your daily activities to suit your natural 'sleep–wake' body rhythm.

If sleep is a problem, try to examine critically exactly what the issues are that prevent you from getting a restful night's sleep and the strategies you may use to overcome it.

EXERCISE

Regular exercise can not only help you to get fit, but can also be a useful way to 'work off' tension and boredom, especially if you are spending most of your day at a desk or sitting down in one spot. Participating in team sports can help you to broaden your social network, which may take your mind off your stressors and anxiety symptoms.

People who are physically fit also tend to sleep better than those who have not been getting regular exercise.

DIET

A well-balanced, healthy diet is crucial to maintaining good physical and mental health. Low blood-sugar levels or certain vitamin deficiencies can make you feel tired or run down and vulnerable to stress symptoms. Too much coffee, tea, cola drinks or foods containing large amounts of chocolate or sugar may leave you feeling 'hyped up'.

Because nicotine (in cigarettes) is a stimulant, smok-ing can also increase your feelings of anxiety – apart from seriously affecting your physical health. If you are a smoker, consider cutting down or quitting as part of your overall stress management programme.

Many people who suffer from anxiety report that small amounts of alcohol help them to cope, especially in social situations. Unfortunately, the regular use of alcohol to control anxiety is counterproductive in the long term as it is easy to become dependent and then to suffer from serious withdrawal symptoms. Furthermore, regular alcohol use can lead to a number of medical complications, some of which may be life-threatening.

PHYSICAL RELAXATION

This is often a neglected area of stress management. While it is important to be concerned about getting enough sleep, exercise and healthy food, it is equally important to consider regular physical relaxation as part of an overall plan for anxiety management. Relaxing by the beach, fishing, going to the movies or getting a massage can all be useful to revitalise those tired muscles and relieve your mind of stress. Another method of relaxing is to practise progressive muscle relaxation, a technique taught over several sessions of instructions designed to help you achieve a deep state of relaxation. This technique helps to get rid of the daily build-up of unpleasant muscle tension. If you suffer from panic attacks, learning to slow your breathing down may also help to reduce your overall arousal level. For further guidance on dealing with panic attacks, consult the book *Overcoming Panic* by Vijaya Manicavasagar and Derrick Silove in this series.

Improving your mental health

The key ingredients in improving your psychological health are to learn how to become more goal-directed, to manage your time more efficiently and to solve your day-to-day problems in a systematic way. Furthermore, mental stress can often be reduced by examining how accurately you are interpreting stressful situations and by challenging any irrational negative perceptions of yourself.

GOAL-SETTING

This is a useful skill that ensures that you prioritise your tasks and acknowledge your successes when you achieve your goals. Try setting yourself small daily goals at first, then work up to the larger goals that may have been worrying you for some time.

TIME MANAGEMENT

Just as important as goal-setting is being able to allocate enough time to yourself to achieve those goals. In fact, these two tasks often go hand in hand. Make sure that when you set yourself realistic goals, you have also allowed yourself enough time to achieve them.

PROBLEM-SOLVING

Not all of us are good at problem-solving. For many of us, this is a skill that may require instruction and regular practice. Effective problem-solving involves first identifying the actual problem; then considering as many solutions as possible, no matter how strange or outrageous they seem; and then weighing up the pros and cons of each solution before selecting a particular answer or answers to your problem.

Implementing and reviewing the outcome of your solution will help you assess whether your problem is indeed solved or whether you need to consider other related problems. Try this strategy of problem-solving first on small problems, then work up to larger ones that may be made up of several smaller worries.

CHALLENGING AND CHANGING NEGATIVE THINKING STYLES

This skill will be addressed further in later steps, and so we will only touch upon it briefly here. In essence, it involves, first, identifying any consistently negative ways in which you may be interpreting stressful situations; then actively challenging those irrational thoughts or perceptions; and finally changing these negative thoughts to positive, more appropriate perceptions that do not generate high levels of distress.

Review of Step 4

Ideally, you should avoid contact with anything to do with gambling. Of course, this is not really possible because there is so much reference to gambling in everyday life – in the media, in advertising and in topics of conversation with friends and colleagues at work and socially. Tablets and smartphones are always close at hand and represent an opportunity to gamble. Nevertheless, it is important that you reduce as far as possible any contact with cues related to gambling.

The urge to gamble can be triggered by cues in the environment (external cues) or by negative emotions and worry (internal cues). List the situations you commonly come across in your everyday activities that remind you of gambling. Write down realistic strategies that you can use to help you avoid contact with these situations. Brainstorm these strategies with your partner or others. Often they provide creative and inspirational suggestions that can be highly effective. They may offer additional suggestions that you did not think of. Plan ahead by preparing a series of steps that you may take if you suddenly find yourself confronted with a situation that is going to trigger your gambling urge. For example, how will you excuse yourself from a conversation if the topic turns to gambling? What can you say?

Identify the internal stresses that cause you to try to escape into a world of gambling. Learn to become aware of, and overcome, negative emotional states before they take hold of you. Do not cope by immersing yourself in gambling. This is an escape that will bring only temporary relief, if not actually aggravate the problem. Rather, learn to tackle the source of stress using effective stress management techniques. Use relaxation methods to reduce high levels of physical tension; practise expressing your concerns to others with the aim of listening to advice on how to handle situations; improve your health by paying attention to sleep, diet, exercise and relaxation so that your physical health is strengthened. Good health is a good foundation for coping with stress.

Step 5

Identifying irrational ideas: how to stop chasing losses

Step 1 of this self-help guide started off by exploring your motivation to stop gambling. In Step 2, you learnt how to monitor your behaviour to become aware of the way in which certain situations act to influence your thinking and gambling behaviour. Having set the stage, you then, in Step 3, learnt a useful relaxation technique, designed to reduce your urge to gamble, which you could easily put into effect when actually confronted by cues in your environment. In Step 4 we moved on to consider the types of triggers operating in your environment and your own emotions that arouse the urge to gamble and ultimately set you on the course toward excessive gambling.

In this Step 5, we are going to examine closely your attitudes and belief structures related to various aspects of gambling and behaviour: that is, what does gambling mean to you, and how does your attitude influence your behaviour?

The importance of beliefs, thoughts and attitudes

Why are beliefs, thoughts and attitudes an important area to deal with? There is an approach to treatment in clinical psychology called 'cognitive therapy'. While there are many strands of cognitive therapy, they all operate on one fundamental premise. This is that cognitions – that is, any mental event that takes place in our minds: images, thoughts, beliefs, memories and attitudes – have a direct influence on our emotions and behaviours. Superstitious behaviour is a good example of how our beliefs cause us to behave and feel in certain ways. Think back on your reactions and how you behaved when you last walked under a ladder, spilt salt or had a black cat walk in front of you. Next time you are gambling, take time to observe the people around you. Often, people playing the slot machines will touch the side of the machine, press the button a certain way or hold some item as a lucky charm. People believe that acting in this way increases their chances of winning.

As an exercise, write down here what attitudes and beliefs you hold about gambling – for instance, 'I believe it is possible to come out a winner', 'My skills at gambling are better than the average gambler's', 'Gambling is a way of making easy money'.

OVERCOMING GAMBLING ADDICTION

Personal beliefs and attitudes about gambling	
1.	
2.	
3.	
4.	
5.	

Cognitions are not isolated bits of mental activity. Rather, they interact to form a general view or 'schema' of the world, a map that you use to process all the pieces of information surrounding you and gather these into a meaningful whole. This map is then used as a guide in how you see yourself, the world around you and your future. People have a tendency to filter out from their environment what they don't want to see and focus only on what they want to see and that which is in keeping with their expectations. If you have a view of yourself as unable to control events in your life, a failure and unloved by others, you will tend to have low self-confidence and be unhappy. How we see ourselves and the world plays a powerful role in shaping our behaviour.

To illustrate, let us consider two people in exactly the same situation, playing electronic gaming machines. One person holds a set of beliefs that he is lucky, that gambling is an easy way of earning additional income and that the only way he can impress others is by showing off success through smart cars and other fancy possessions. In contrast, the other person sees gambling as a form of entertainment, a leisure activity that he enjoys playing to pass the time. He sees himself as a hard worker who values effort, is confident in his own abilities and is not concerned about what others think of him. The attitudes each holds will determine how he behaves.

With the first person, winning is an important source of self-esteem. A win will boost his ego, it will reinforce the belief that one can win gambling and increase the likelihood of his boasting to others. A loss will undermine this feeling, resulting in further gambling to recapture the ego boost. For the second, a win or loss will have little impact on his ego, mood or behaviour because of his low expectation of winning. He will more readily accept losing without becoming emotionally upset.

In cognitive therapy, the aim is to work out the set of distorted and irrational cognitions – thoughts, attitudes, beliefs – we have, challenge their accuracy and replace them with more rational and accurate cognitions. Thus the first step we need to take is to identify distorted and mistaken perceptions of gambling. Having done this, we can challenge those perceptions by critically examining what evidence we have to support our views; we are then in a position to replace them with more accurate perceptions. Correcting erroneous and faulty cognitions is another step in the right direction in overcoming problem gambling.

Let us begin by looking at some of the more common irrational cognitions held by people who gamble.

Common cognitive distortions and erroneous beliefs in problem gambling

Gambling: Entertainment or a source of income?

A fundamental question to ask yourself is this: Does gambling represent a way of earning income or is it a form of entertainment?

Gamblers who hold the mistaken belief that gambling is a way of making money will:

- feel bad when they lose;
- chase their losses;
- overestimate their gambling abilities and skills and so take greater risks;
- be prepared to risk more than they can afford on tips or 'certainties';
- become preoccupied with thoughts of gambling;
- gamble rather than work to save money for purchases or payment of bills.

Gamblers who correctly understand that gambling is a costly form of entertainment will:

- be prepared to accept losing in exchange for having a good time;
- not chase losses;
- recognise that gambling involves minimal skill on their part;
- limit the amount of money risked to what they can afford;
- think little of gambling at other times;
- save rather than gamble to obtain needed cash.

Don't be misled by friends who claim that they consistently win. They are still working for a living and are unlikely to boast about their losses. To overcome your gambling, you have to accept the fact that gambling is really entertainment. Essentially, you are paying the gambling industry a fee for the privilege of using some of their facilities to get a sense of excitement and fun. Occasionally they may offer an inducement to continue gambling in the form of a win, simply to encourage you to keep coming back. Do not use terms such as 're-investing your winnings in gambling'. You are not investing anything; you are spending money to purchase a product, that is, entertainment, in the guise of a chance to obtain a return, even if it is less than what you paid for it.

'I can win at gambling'

The most prominent erroneous belief among gamblers – and perhaps the hardest to shift – is that you can win at gambling. This fantasy is encouraged by media reports of instant lottery millionaires and big-time casino or race winners, as well as personal experience of winning. True, people can be lucky and have a large win. But examine closely what happens over a period of time. Sadly, most winners return the money through further gambling. Stories abound of lottery winners who, in a very short space of time, either spend or gamble their money away to be left penniless.

I often hear gamblers I have treated say, in referring to a recent large win, 'See, there's the evidence. I won last week, I can do it again.' A nineteen-year-old unemployed adolescent won the equivalent of fifty thousand pounds on a trifecta (picking the first three horses in order) at a trotting meeting in Sydney. Within two weeks, he had lost the lot. He then reported that he 'went out of control' trying to recover his money, and ended up the equivalent of ten thousand pounds in debt, having been convinced, on the basis of one major win, that he could repeat his success.

To examine your own beliefs about gambling and winning, consider the following case.

Trevor has played the slot machines twice a week for the last five years. He invests ten pounds and comes out with, on average, five pounds left in his pocket after each session. At the last session he again started with ten pounds, but halfway through he won a jackpot of a thousand pounds. In his excitement he extended his session, finally stopping when he had only three hundred pounds left in his pocket. Over the next three days he returned and lost the remaining three hundred pounds.

Now, write down your responses to the following questions:

Did Trevor win at gambling?....................................

Did Trevor win overall during the week? ....

Has Trevor been winning over the long term? ....

Your answers to these questions will depend on what you mean by winning.

If we limit the time frame to one session, did Trevor win a thousand pounds or what he had left at the end of the session, that is, three hundred pounds?

And what happens when we extend the time frame? If we take into account his performance over three days, can we still say that he won, given the fact that he had returned the thousand pounds by that stage?

What about if we extend the time frame to cover the last twelve months? He has consistently lost 50 per cent of his stake. How much did he lose before winning a thousand pounds briefly – which he then gave back?

Take a few minutes to explore what winning means to you. Focusing on the outcome of a single bet, such as Trevor's thousand-pound jackpot in the above example, will reinforce for you the idea that large wins are possible. This will also foster an impression that such a win places you financially ahead. How many times have you heard someone boast of a large win? What they fail to report is how much they had in their hand at the end of the session. Remember: it doesn't matter how much you win during one session, whether it's a million pounds or more; the crucial questions are how much did you start with and how much did you finish with? Those are the key facts.

Rather than focusing on individual sessions only, you must monitor your gambling so that you can then calculate your position in regard to wins and losses over a minimum period of twelve months. The longer the time frame, the more losses you will have. That's the nature of gambling.

Next time someone boasts of winning, ask how much money they lost trying to gain that win. A friend of mine excitedly reported that he had won five hundred pounds on a horse race. His face paled when I asked him how much he had bet and lost in the previous races that day and in the preceding week. His elation turned to dejection when he calculated that he had lost seven hundred and fifty pounds to win five hundred!

The illusion of control

Chance plays a central role in gambling. However, many gamblers hold a strong conviction that they can influence the outcome of chance events through their own skilful play. This observation was first reported by E. J. Langer, a researcher who in 1975 carried out experiments that confirmed her hypothesis. She found that people consistently over-estimated their ability to influence the outcome of a chance event, even though their skill had absolutely no part to play in determining the final result. We just like to think we have special skills over and above the next gambler.

Take a moment to write down any strategies you follow that you believe give you the winning edge. Review these to see how many are based on real skill and how many are merely superstitious beliefs. To illustrate, gamblers playing craps may throw the dice hard when aiming for high numbers and softly to secure low numbers. In poker, gamblers may arrange the cards in a certain way, slowly revealing the cards one at a time. Lottery players may select favourite numbers. Horse race bettors are renowned for having 'systems' that are guaranteed to beat the bookies. In reality, however hard or softly you toss the dice, however you handle the cards, whatever your favourite number or system you employ, none of these so-called skills influences the outcome one little bit.

What are some of the factors that strengthen our sense of illusion of control? Three have been suggested by Robert Ladouceur and the late Michael Walker, colleagues and international experts in understanding gambling behaviour: these are competition, familiarity and choice.

COMPETITION

Competition is usually based on the exercise of skill. Therefore, if you challenge an opponent and win, you automatically assume the win to be the result of your personal skill, not of good luck on your part.

FAMILIARITY

The more familiar you are with a machine, casino, race-track or lottery office, the more likely are you to believe that you have control over the outcome. Do you have a favourite slot machine or purchase lottery tickets from a regular agent? Are you drawn to a particular fruit or slot machine because you 'know the spin of the reel'? This is increasingly relevant in sports betting. Many sports bettors follow their team and are familiar with the players. There is the emotional tension to remain loyal and keep betting on them. Familiarity in these cases often leads to bad decisions.

ACTIVE PARTICIPATION AND CHOICE

It has been shown that people value lottery tickets that they have chosen themselves over and above those that have been given to them by an agent. So, if you are able to select numbers or tickets, you are more likely to have more confidence in winning.

I have had numerous debates with problem gamblers over the issue of skills and systems. They argue, somewhat illogically, that they have the necessary skills or systems to win, but are prevented from coming out ahead by a run of 'bad luck' or some other reason. They point to a recent succession of wins over a brief period of time, which in their mind confirms their belief. Think about the robust debates over a pint of beer about sports betting, be it horses, soccer, tennis or cricket. Each person believes they have the skills to pick their winning team.

Take a moment to think about the following points:

- Gambling is not a competition to prove anything to anyone. What does 'beating the system' really mean? Ask yourself, what are you proving to whom if you win at gambling?
- One or two runs of wins does not prove skill or the effectiveness of a system.
- Pure chance with no skill can result in a series of wins.
- If you have the skills to win, can you explain why you are in debt? It is no good explaining that it is due to bad luck.
- If wins are the result of your skill, then losing must also be the result of your skill (or lack of it). Overall, what is your ratio of wins to losses? If you have lost more than you have won, what does this say about your skill?
- Carrying a lucky charm has no impact on chance events; it is only superstitious behaviour.

No matter how strongly you hold the cognitive belief that you are a skilful player, the outcome of gambling is determined by chance, over which you have no influence whatsoever. The skill of the poker player or horse-race gambler is not in consistently winning but in knowing when to cut their losses.

Biased evaluation

A phenomenon related to the illusion of control is that of biased evaluations. People do not like to think that they have no skill or ability to pick winners. It makes you feel proud and boosts your ego if others perceive you as a 'skilful' gambler, one who is consistently likely to be ahead, one who knows how to 'read the signs'. So, what do you do when you lose? Easy – you blame someone or something else: the machine is 'fixed', the jockey 'pulled the horse' or the team deliberately 'threw the game'. You take credit for picking winners and dismiss the losses by blaming some outside cause. How many times have you heard fellow gamblers complaining about 'fluke' events that led to losses while boasting of their skills when winning? This biased approach to explaining outcomes means that you tend to remember wins and attribute them to your skills, while losses are quickly and easily put aside and forgotten.

Listen to others who play cards or bet on sports. How often have you heard them say that their cards, selected team or horse should have won had it not been for the last card turned being the one they did not expect to come up, or that the referees made bad calls, or the jockey deliberately pulled the horse? This is common in online forms of gambling, where losses are attributed to the operator fixing software or the payback percentage.

As an exercise, fill in the list here with the last five wins you had. Describe how much, and where, you won. Now make a similar list for your last five losses. Can you remember these as easily?

Wins		Losses	
How much won	Where won	How much lost	Where lost
1.			
2.			
3.			
4.			
5.			

Try explaining why you lost in each case. Write the reasons down on the list next to the column describing where you lost.

Near-wins

How many times have the symbols on a slot machine lined up for a jackpot except for one crucial reel, your horse lost by a short head or the lottery result come in just one or two digits different from your ticket? Have you noticed how such 'near-wins' increase your expectation that a win is about due, and how this spurs you on to continue gambling?

Comments often heard from gamblers include:

- 'I'm almost there, one or two more plays and the jackpot must come up.'
- 'The machine is about to start paying, I must keep going.'
- 'Gee, my luck is about to change, I can't stop now.'
- 'Wow, that was close, the next one must win.'

Near-misses, also called 'heart-stoppers', are almost as exciting as actual wins. But don't be deceived. In reality, missing by a whisker is the same as a missing by a mile. It doesn't matter if you needed only the ace on the first reel to win a million or that your horse lost by a nose. The end result is that you lost. More importantly, the results have absolutely no bearing on the next event. Events in gambling are independent. By this I mean that the result of one event has no effect in influencing the next. The roulette spins a number, say 26. The probability of 26 coming up again is exactly the same for the next spin. This occurred to me when I was visiting a casino in Australia with my wife during a conference. I placed a chip on a number, which came up. Distracted by a conversation with my wife, I left the chips on the same number, which again came up. The same happened again on the next spin. At that stage, we decided that we had won enough to satisfy us, that to continue would inevitably lead to our losing what we had won. So we cashed in our wins and enjoyed a great dinner.

Gambling to get out of debt

Look at it logically. Gambling has been the direct cause of the financial problems now facing you. You have gambled for several years and are well behind. What makes you think that gambling is the answer to your problems? What has changed that gives you the idea that you will win now? It is irrational to think that gambling can be a solution to your financial problems when your experience clearly demonstrates that it is the very cause of those problems!

Another, related, erroneous cognition is reflected in the following argument.

My gambling has caused a major financial problem. I have debts that I cannot pay and I do not have enough money to pay my bills and daily living expenses. I have only a few pounds left, which is not going to make any impact on reducing the debt or paying the bills. I owe two hundred pounds but have only twenty; what difference will twenty pounds make in paying off my debt? However, I could win two hundred pounds by gambling that twenty pounds – so why not try? I have nothing to lose. What's the difference between owing two hundred pounds and owing two hundred and twenty? But if I win two hundred pounds, just imagine, my problem would be solved.

In fact, research has shown that even winning does not solve a gambler's financial problems. Following a major win, gamblers are reluctant to pay off debts. Rather, they reserve the money for future gambling.

> *I am on a winning streak. If I continue, I will be able to win enough not only to pay off present debts but also to be able to continue gambling and still have enough to pay bills that are due shortly.*

The inevitable result is that you lose not only your available cash but also your winnings, leaving you in an even worse position.

Even if you pay off the existing debts from a win, within a short time you will repeat the cycle by creating more debts through continued gambling, which plunges you back into debt.

Has either of these situations applied to you?

Gambling is an illness over which I have no control

Many people find it too threatening to admit that they choose to engage in a behaviour that causes harm to themselves or others. It is far easier to avoid responsibility by laying blame on some external cause of the behaviour, such as an illness or addiction. Frequently heard excuses are:

- I had no control over my behaviour.
- The addiction to gambling is too strong to resist.
- I am suffering from a compulsive gambling illness.
- The urge totally overwhelmed me.

Make a list of all the reasons you can think of why you are unable to resist the urge to gamble.

1 ....

2 ....

3 ....

4 ....

5 ....

6 ....

7 ....

8 ....

How many of these reasons are genuine explanations for lack of control over your behaviour? I suspect none. It is all too easy to refer to gambling as an addiction or illness under the spell of which you are completely powerless: 'Don't blame me, I can't help it, it's not my fault.' This is wrong. Even though your gambling problem may be an addiction or illness (although this is still hotly debated among the experts), this does not diminish the role you play in making your own choices. One cannot argue, as you may with alcohol or drug addiction, that the body has a physiological craving for a substance and it is this need that you are fulfilling. Gambling is not associated with any bodily need, only a sense of excitement. You must admit that you gamble because you enjoy the feeling, because you are stressed or want to escape unpleasant moods.

Think hard: can you identify any virus or bacterium that causes gambling? No; there is no such thing. There may be some biological factors that might make you more vulnerable to respond to rewards more than compared to others. But this does not hijack your capacity to make decisions. Gambling is a repetitive behaviour that one chooses to engage in despite the unpleasant consequences that result. It takes courage to confront the truth and accept that you are voluntarily giving in to the urge to gamble because you want to gamble even though it may harm you. But once you take this step, you are taking responsibility for your actions and not blaming outside sources. You are now regaining control over your life.

Suggestions on how to challenge erroneous and irrational beliefs

We have spent some time here describing the types of erroneous and irrational cognitions that some people hold which make them more vulnerable to losing control. Your next step is to learn how to challenge these cognitions and turn them into positive thoughts.

This involves critically examining each thought and considering how accurate it is. To do this, you need to look closely at and challenge the evidence that you think may support your belief. For example, if you believe that you can make money from gambling to pay bills, you should ask yourself the following questions: 'Where is the evidence that I can actually make money? How many times in the past have I actually won and used that money to pay the bill?' or: 'I feel confident that I will win on this occasion, but how many times have I felt this way before and ended up still losing?'

Try challenging some of your thoughts by completing the exercise set out overleaf. Look at the two situations in the example and try to recall the thoughts you had under similar circumstances. Are they rational? If not, why not? What is a more realistic view? Write down a few typical thoughts that occur when you have the urge to gamble in particular situations, and then write down the challenge to them.

The next stage in overcoming irrational thoughts is to replace the erroneous thoughts you have identified with rational, positive thoughts that will improve your sense of self-control and confidence. You should challenge the evidence that leads you to think that you are in the grip of an irresistible urge that you cannot control no matter what. Rather, you should come to realise that you are in fact making a voluntary choice, even though the choice may be a bad one. Let's work through an example. After that, complete the exercise by adding your own examples in the spaces provided.

Situation	Irrational thought	Challenging the evidence in support
1 Finishing a hard day's work and feeling tense and stressed.	I have had a stressful day. To unwind I will drop in and play the slot machines for an hour and no more. I'll gamble five pounds and no more.	How many times in the past have I intended to limit the time and amount gambled but lost control? The end result is that I am more tense and unhappy, not relaxed, after those sessions.
2 Playing the slot machines. Because of a few near-wins, anticipating a win.	There were a number of close calls. Carrying out a ritual such as touching the side of the machine before inserting the coin will improve my chances.	I have carried out my ritual many times before under the same circumstances and it has made no difference.
3		
4		

Think back to the last time you were in a gambling situation and the thoughts that were passing through your mind. First, describe the situation.

Situation: Walking past a shop selling lottery tickets, a casino or betting office and having a strong urge to enter.

Now write down any irrational thoughts that entered your mind, whether they relate to overestimating your level of skill, superstitious behaviour or the way you usually talk to yourself in such situations.

Irrational thoughts: The last time I bought a ticket, played a table game, gaming machine or placed a bet it was only one number or winning icon off winning a prize, or I just lost by a nose. I could win this time. The urge is too strong for me to resist, I must buy a ticket.

What can you say to yourself to challenge these irrational thoughts? Ask yourself, 'Where is the objective evidence to support what I am thinking?'

Challenging irrational thoughts: How many times in the past have I been close and still never won the next time? The result of one draw, picking a number or horse has no effect on the results of any other draw, spin of a roulette wheel or race. Just because I came close to a winning outcome does not mean that the chance of winning is increased for any future bets that I place. I do have the choice of betting or not betting; nobody is forcing me to go and buy a ticket.

Now try to substitute thoughts that are rational and reflect reality. What do you consider is the real situation, rather than the situation as you wish it were? What can you say to yourself that will help you realise and accept the truth that you can control your urges and behaviours and make good choices?

Positive thoughts: I can control my urge when I accept that it is my choice to gamble or not. I feel good when I decide to keep the money and not squander it on an unrealistic hope.

Identifying irrational thoughts and seeing them for what they are – false beliefs that lead to bad choices and further suffering from gambling – takes a lot of effort and practice. However, with experience you will be able to challenge erroneous thoughts and substitute positive ones that will improve your self-esteem and ability to overcome your problem gambling. Try the process as described above with some situations of your own in the spaces provided here.

IDENTIFYING IRRATIONAL IDEAS

Situation: ....
....
Irrational thoughts: ....
....
Challenging thoughts: ....
....
Positive thoughts: ....
....

Situation: ....
....
Irrational thoughts: ....
....
Challenging thoughts: ....
....
Positive thoughts: ....
....

Situation: ....
....
Irrational thoughts: ....
....
Challenging thoughts: ....
....
Positive thoughts: ....
....

Review of Step 5

This step has addressed some of the different types of thinking errors that gamblers often engage in. By now, you should be aware that the attitudes and beliefs you have held regarding gambling as a source of income, a game at which you can win, a solution to financial problems and a behaviour over which you have no control are all erroneous. Remember, the more accurate your perception is of what gambling is really all about, the greater will be your motivation to stop. Do not accept people's boasting at face value; challenge them by seeking more information on their true position in relation to how much they have won or lost overall.

Questioning your own 'positive' views toward gambling will help you eventually overcome your habit. Recognising that the only real winners in gambling are the gambling industry and the government, who reap the benefits of your losses, will help strengthen your resolve to give up.

Review your progress by answering the following questions:

- Can you identify what erroneous beliefs led you to think you could win in the long term?
- Have you studied the strategies the gambling industry use to entice you to continue gambling?
- Have you started focusing on your losses rather than emphasising your wins?

- Are you able to challenge your view that gambling is a solution to cash problems?
- Have you accepted responsibility for your own behaviour?

If you can answer 'yes' to these questions, you have made further progress toward overcoming your problem gambling.

Step 6

Preventing relapses

Once you have learnt the skills described in the earlier steps, you need to maintain the gains you have achieved. This is done simply by regular practice and review, and by anticipating danger signals so that you can act quickly to prevent any recurrence of gambling behaviour. The slide back into problem gambling can be an insidious process; outwardly innocent decisions that you make can slowly lead you into high-risk situations. Once exposed to gambling cues, especially if you are under stress and suffering unpleasant emotions, thoughts of having a small fling easily enter your mind. Having one or two small bets can give the false impression that you have full control over the problem and can now safely indulge on occasions without concern. Excuses are made that allow you into more contact with gambling situations, for example by entering gambling establishments with others or by discussing gambling topics in conversations with colleagues. Unfortunately, experience has shown that it is only a matter of time before you find yourself staking more than you intended, or an amount that you can ill afford. This sets off the pressure to have a further bet to catch up. Then comes the chasing as one falls increasingly behind in bills; the downward cycle to relapse has begun.

In this step, you will learn skills in planning ahead and in avoiding risk situations that may precipitate a relapse.

Keeping the long view

The path to recovery is often bumpy; there are bound to be ups and downs as you struggle to regain control over problem gambling habits. Keep your eye on the overall picture and do not dwell on lapses. Lapses do occur; often they are just individual hiccups, rather than signs of failure and complete relapse. A relapse, on the other hand, is where old habits repeatedly return and take over.

A lapse – that is, a brief return to gambling, be it one bet, a session over several hours or a few episodes of gambling – is a warning sign cautioning you that you need to be more vigilant in practising and applying the skills you have learnt. Re-reading this book and renewing your efforts may be all that is required to get you back into step. At other times, it may be necessary to get straight in touch with your family doctor or counsellor – for example if you are facing additional problems of depression or overwhelming stresses. Do not be despondent in the face of a lapse.

Whether or not you succeed in the long term depends on how you respond to these hiccups. Take the approach that each hiccup is a cautionary warning not to become complacent; when it happens, going through this book again is strongly recommended. I like to use the example of dieting when discussing this point with my clients. Having embarked on a diet, one is invited out to dinner. During the course of the meal, one eats a plate of chocolate dessert. If one feels guilty about this, one may become depressed, seeing it as a complete failure to control the desire to eat sweets, and give up trying any further. The consequence of this is that one will resume overeating and gain weight. A relapse has occurred. Alternatively, one could see the initial event as a lapse and decide that compensatory action needs to be applied; having eaten dessert, plans are made to reduce the intake at the next meal or to exercise more the following day. Planning ahead serves to restore the balance and averts a relapse.

To anticipate and avoid lapses, one needs to:

- be aware of what may cause the return of an urge to gamble;
- understand the series of apparently irrelevant decisions that leads to exposure to gambling opportunities;
- be familiar with the steps needed to avoid or contain damage.

Guarding against the urge to gamble

Generally speaking, urges do not enter our minds suddenly and spontaneously. A number of factors, singly or in combination, may contribute to the appearance of an urge: the most common ones are unpleasant moods and emotions, arguments or conflict with others, and peer pressure. Also, pleasant and/or unexpected events, moods, and exposure to gambling promotions, offers of freebies or bonus bets, or free play can stimulate urges.

Unpleasant moods or emotions

A gambling lapse can occur in response to the following moods:

- depression, unhappiness or feeling low;
- a sense of frustration in achieving goals;
- resentment at missing out on recognition, praise or promotion for work completed;
- boredom;
- worry and anxiety;
- rejection by others;
- low self-esteem and self-confidence;
- feelings of worthlessness;
- feelings of impatience;
- failure to meet one's unrealistic expectations;
- a sense of failing to achieve one's ambitions.

Which of these apply to you?

For some people, it seems that a swing to elation or euphoria can also be involved, particularly when it is associated with feelings of overconfidence and grandiose ideas that affect judgment.

Interpersonal conflicts

Arguments with one's spouse or partner, family members, friends or employers can create tensions and unpleasant moods, causing one to seek escape through gambling. Gambling is used to discharge tension and as a distraction from pain in much the same way as alcohol or drugs are used to deaden the pain of anxiety. Some common sources of interpersonal conflict include:

- arguments over finances, for example lack of money to buy necessities, go on holidays or buy new items for home or family;
- loss of affection between partners;
- marital sexual dissatisfaction, tension or infidelity;
- criticism of inadequate effort at work or around the home;
- unrealistic expectations;
- being unreliable;
- receiving inadequate attention from a partner – a common feeling following the birth of a baby;
- not getting on with in-laws;

- external conflicts spilling over into one's marital relationship;
- rivalry between peers at work;
- personality clashes with one's boss or colleagues;
- jealousy over the achievements or praise of others.

Again, consider whether any of these apply to you.

Peer and social pressure

Mixing with acquaintances and peers who are active gamblers and who spend a lot of time talking about gambling-related topics is risky. Being constantly reminded of gambling and hearing of large wins by others can gradually undermine your decision not to gamble. Of even more concern is the pressure to agree to invitations to visit gambling establishments.

Ask yourself:

- Do you feel powerless in the face of peer pressure to gamble?
- Do you feel that your acquaintances will laugh or be critical of you if you refuse to participate in the conversation or go with them to gamble?
- Do you fear becoming socially isolated?

It is difficult to control the urge once surrounded by all the glitter and opportunity. It is not in your best interest to protect such social acquaintances at all cost; if all else fails, you may have to face the painful decision whether to continue to mix socially with people who gamble, and so put yourself at risk, or to establish a new circle of friends.

What can you do? The following is recommended:

- Inform your acquaintances of your problem and your decision to stop gambling.
- Ask them not to talk about gambling in your presence.
- Suggest alternative places to go for lunch or a drink. There are eating and drinking places around that do not allow gambling on the premises.
- Ask them to keep an eye on you in regard to gambling. Few things are more effective than knowing others are watching and supervising your behaviour.
- Agree to the suggestion that they inform your partner should they spot you gambling.

If your acquaintances ridicule you, or are in any way not supportive of your efforts to overcome your gambling, they are people not worth socialising with. A true friend will endeavour to support you in any way possible, even it means a degree of inconvenience to them. Value these people, because you can turn to them for encouragement at times of need.

Hints on dealing with dangerous situations

Spend a few minutes considering these mood states, conflict situations and peer pressures and write down a list of possible positive actions you can apply to overcome them. Have a brainstorm session with your partner to see what alternative strategies are available. Think of as many alternatives as possible, no matter how ridiculous or unrealistic they may seem. Write down responses you could make to colleagues who are enticing you to join them gambling. Use your imagination. Once you have exhausted your thoughts, review them and select the ones you believe could be useful. Make a shortlist ranked in order of how important they are to you. Write these down on a small index card that you can keep in your wallet or purse and take out as a reminder whenever you experience one of these moods, conflicts or peer pressures. In this way, you will have the response to the threat immediately to hand.

Avoiding accidental exposure to high-risk situations

It is rare that one will deliberately place oneself in a high-risk situation – that is, one where the possibility of a lapse is greater than normal, for example, visiting a pub where there are electronic gaming devices, or reading a form guide 'just to see who won, out of interest'. Usually, a chain of small and apparently innocent or irrelevant decisions are made that, when put together, result in a lapse. What is happening is that, unconsciously, you are setting yourself up for a lapse. A few typical such decisions are presented below for you to consider. Study these and see which ones are relevant for you.

- I won't gamble, I just want to join my colleagues for a few drinks at the pub.
- I would like to go into the betting shop to test my control. I'm confident I'll succeed.
- I haven't had the urge now for days so there's no problem in my carrying all this cash.
- I've got a few hours to kill, I'll just drop into my favourite club or casino, have a few drinks and watch others play the machines or table games.
- There's no need to rush home after work, I'll drop into the club/casino for a while and unwind instead.
- I want to listen to the race broadcast to see how a horse I know has run its race. I don't care what price it came in at, I'm interested only in its performance.
- My partner and I are arguing. I'll just spend a few pence playing the machines to relax and put myself into a better frame of mind.

It is easy to justify one decision as being totally unrelated to any desire to gamble. There is nothing wrong with carrying around cash in your pocket. There is nothing wrong with visiting friends for lunch. There is basically nothing wrong with watching friends play the slot machines for fun. But put all these together and you have a recipe for disaster. How long do you think you will be able to resist the urge if you are watching others enjoy playing and winning while you stand around with spare cash in your pocket, particularly if you are feeling down in the dumps and under pressure to pay bills?

Review your monitoring sheets to see if there is any consistent pattern in your behaviour. Now see if there are any statements that you make to justify your decision to approach a gambling situation, and think of alternative things you could do that would avoid exposure to gambling cues. For example, you could meet friends somewhere else or visit other friends away from a pub or club; you could arrange to meet your partner immediately after work, or resolve your conflict with your partner directly rather than using it as an excuse to start gambling. It is important that you look at each and every decision to pinpoint what the likely outcome might be. In this way, you can recognise the early danger signs signalling the imminence of a lapse.

Hints on avoiding unintended exposure to risk

On a series of index cards, list alternative actions to follow under all the circumstances you may inadvertently find yourself facing. Describe all these preventive actions in detail, step by step. Learn to be honest with yourself; there is no point in persuading yourself that you can control a situation when in reality you are really setting yourself up for failure. The only person you are letting down is yourself.

Consider whether your motivation is flagging. If you think it is, re-motivate yourself by returning to Step 1 and reviewing the reasons why you should stop gambling. If necessary, resume monitoring gambling behaviour more intensely to find out if there are any new stresses you are having difficulty dealing with. A revision of problem-solving and stress management skills (Step 4) can be effective in boosting your ability to cope with anxiety and other negative emotions. Go back to regular practice of the relaxation-based imaginal desensitisation procedure (Step 3). Construct a new sequence specific to the new situation and record a new set of instructions. Now go back to Step 4 and refresh your skills in challenging irrational beliefs and distorted thinking styles.

What can be done to minimise or contain damage?

What does one do if faced with an impending lapse? When, say, you have just started playing the slots, table games, begun studying the form guide or purchased a lottery ticket? Stop: don't put in the next coin, place the next bet or buy any more tickets. Take a few minutes' time out to slow yourself down. Take out your index card that has written on it: 'Even though I am happy and confident now, how will I feel WHEN I LOSE?' and give yourself at least three good reasons why you should not continue to gamble. Write these down for future reference if you can.

A note of caution if your goal of treatment is abstinence. Quite often people pursuing abstinence use the proverbial excuse to keep going on, 'I might as well be hung for a sheep as for a lamb', suggesting that the degree to which they gamble is of no relevance. Saying 'I have started gambling, oh well, I might as well carry on now' is absolutely no justification for your behaviour. This is the very point at which you must redouble your efforts in applying all the relapse prevention strategies described above.

Once you have got out of the situation, immediately let your partner know of what has just happened. Under no circumstances try to conceal your activity through deceit, covering losses through borrowing or gambling more in the hope of recovering what is lost. Accept responsibility for your error in judgment and the reactions of others toward you. A partner may well be angry at first but he or she will appreciate the fact that you approached him or her for support. In this way, trust will be rebuilt. Most important of all, involving your partner will eliminate any anxiety or pressure on you to gamble as a means of avoiding detection. Invariably, the clients who have responded well to therapy are the ones who have taken the courage to inform their partner, friend or counsellor immediately of any lapse. You will be surprised to see how much worry is lifted off your shoulders once you have disclosed your lapse. But do not abuse this trust and support. A repeated cycle of lapses followed by confessions should raise a question mark over your motivation. If this is happening, be aware that you are manipulating the goodwill of others. A revision of Step 1 is recommended: question your ambivalence or commitment to change.

Review of Step 6

In Step 6 we have considered the importance of anticipating high-risk situations, planning ahead and working out alternative actions to avoid or minimise damage.

- Have you made a list of all the high-risk situations you are most likely to encounter?
- Are you familiar with the chains of individual decisions you make that eventually result in exposing you to such high-risk situations?
- Have you written out a plan of action to follow at any stage when you inadvertently find yourself confronted with an opportunity to gamble?
- Do you know what to say to people who invite or pressure you to join them in a bet?
- Are you in the habit of discussing with your partner or other confidante any urges that may arise, no matter how trivial?

- Are you committed to informing your partner instantly if you have gambled any amount, no matter how small?

If you are confident in answering 'yes' to all of these questions, you are well on the way to maintaining the recovery process in overcoming problem gambling.

Step 7

How your family can help

Many gamblers make the mistake of believing they have to struggle to overcome problem gambling on their own. In fact, it is far more effective to work together with partners and other family members in a cooperative manner. Often, a gambler will shy away from asking for help from a family member because of shame, fear of the consequences or repercussions if the full extent of gambling and debts/losses were revealed, loss of trust, or desire to manage the problem on their own. It is emphasised that taking the first step in eliciting help from family members will go a long way in helping you achieve your goals.

Do not underestimate the extent to which you can be helped by the efforts of others in giving you advice, encouragement and recognition and praise for successes achieved. They can provide you with feedback that will reinforce your motivation and maintain your effort in continuing to pursue your goals, particularly when the going gets tough.

If you are single or separated from your partner, you may wish to turn to your immediate family instead. Parents are usually more than willing to help their children overcome problems and are a good source of help. But do not expect to rely on them to solve all your difficulties or to offer you financial assistance to clear your debts. That is an abuse of their position and trust. It is up to you to develop the skills to handle stresses and take responsibility for your financial situation.

Often, gamblers ask parents or partners to cover their debts, that is, to bail them out of a financial crisis in return for promises of repayment. Once the dust settles, the promises are broken and the cycle repeated. Bailing out a gambler is not a solution; it is only a temporary relief at best and at worst an aggravation of the situation. I recall one client who, in debt to the tune of twelve thousand pounds, asked his girlfriend, with whom he lived, to ask her parents for a loan to repay what he owed. This she did, much to his relief. No gambling took place for the next six months; but then, gradually, he succumbed to the temptation and again began gambling small amounts. The inevitable happened. Confident that he was in control, he began to gamble more and more, and his gambling escalated to the extent that twelve months later he had accumulated a new debt of fifteen thousand pounds. The end result of his partner's good intention in bailing him out was that the couple now owed twenty-seven thousand pounds and were forced to sell some assets they had put aside for their future security.

It was clear that my client had limited insight and poor motivation to cease his gambling. Relieved that he was able to eliminate his debt with a further loan from his girlfriend's parents, it became apparent by his attitude that he had not learnt his lesson. I suspect that currently he is on the slippery slope to a third similar crisis. Had his partner remained firm and provided support and encouragement to seek treatment rather than procuring cash, he would have realised the futility of continued gambling and pursued treatment to the benefit of all concerned.

How can your family contribute to helping you overcome your gambling problem? The following suggestions may be useful:

- Communicate openly with your partner about any stress or problems that are facing you. Adopt a policy of trying to solve problems jointly with her/him.

- Do not keep emotions bottled up inside. Obtain feedback and support from your family in learning how to express emotions more appropriately.

- Contact your partner or a family member whenever you experience an urge to gamble.

- Talk about how you feel and allow your partner to refocus your attention on the reasons why you are giving up or cutting back on the gambling.

- Put into place a contingency plan to follow if an urge persists. This may include arranging for a member of your family to pick you up after work to prevent you visiting a pub or club.

- Work out a budget in cooperation with your partner. It may be necessary for you to receive a weekly allowance for a while until you can prove to others that you are trustworthy. Do not feel resentful at this: it is your behaviour that has led to this need in the first place.

- Monitor your savings and expenditure and have a regular weekly meeting with your partner to discuss progress. In this way you can receive praise for your achievements.

- Consider ways of limiting your access to cash. Allow your partner to confiscate all your credit cards and cheque books. The idea is not to relinquish all responsibility for finances; rather, you need to convince others that you can control your behaviour and can be trusted to meet all your financial commitments. Once this has been accomplished, you can gradually resume responsibility for the family budget.

- If you have gambled, on however small a scale, disclose this to your partner. Again, I repeat that attempting to conceal bets and chase losses to avoid being caught, and the pressure this causes, is the best recipe for failure. Learn to deal directly with failures rather than avoiding them.

- From your monitoring sheets, work out the times of high risk when you are most likely to gamble. Arrange to do alternative activities during those times that will conflict with your ability to gamble. If Saturdays are a bad time, go out to the movies or visit friends. Having something to do will distract you and make it easier to overcome the urge.

- If you have selected controlled gambling as a goal, you will need your partner to act as a supervisor. You must report to her or him each week, showing detailed evidence of the amount you gambled, its source and the outcome in terms of wins and losses. Do not deceive her or him; if you do, eventually you will be discovered and your credibility will be reduced to zero.

- Be prepared, and expect, to have your family scrutinise your every move, to remain suspicious of whether or not you have gambled, and to doubt statements that you are no longer gambling. You cannot blame them for not trusting you; it was your behaviour that undermined their trust in you.

- Finally, accept that your family are concerned about you and that their efforts are all directed toward providing maximum assistance in helping you improve your quality of life by overcoming your problem gambling.

At times, conflict within families over gambling has reached mammoth proportions, resulting in frequent undermining critical comments, arguments and reference to the past: 'It is your fault we have no money, look at how poorly you provide for your family. Even our neighbours on lower salaries do a better job than you. I knew I should have married Joe when I had the chance.' Such comments erode any sense of motivation or self-esteem and make a relapse likely. If there are entrenched difficulties in the relationship, or your partner is showing signs of giving up, it may be necessary for you to consult a marriage or relationship counsellor to address these issues. Threats of separation or divorce should be taken seriously as a sign that your partner has reached the end of her or his tolerance with your behaviour. It is up to you to work cooperatively in establishing an atmosphere of reconciliation and, with the joint effort and support of those around you, in overcoming your problem gambling.

A concluding remark

Voluntarily to give up an activity that provides so much excitement and dreams of potential wealth is always going to be difficult. But there is no easy road to an easy life. If gambling has created difficulties in your life, you can be sure that continued participation is certainly not the way to overcome these problems. With the assistance of family members and others, you can act to improve the quality of your life immeasurably.

There may well be setbacks along the way, but do not give up hope and motivation. Re-read this book at regular intervals and continually renew the skills you have learnt. Practice is essential if you are to gain mastery over your urges. If you find you need additional guidance, consult your local mental health professional. One or more sessions with a professional can complement the principles outlined in this book and can be an excellent preventive measure to avoid a major relapse.

At no stage should you become complacent and assume you are fully in control and able to resume gambling in the same manner as before. Booster sessions of the imaginal desensitisation procedure every six to eight months are recommended as a safety measure.

At all stages be aware that you are overcoming problem gambling for your own sake, but that you are doing so in cooperation with your partner and family members. Seek as much external support as possible. Do not hesitate to call upon your loved ones to provide encouragement and support. Receiving recognition and praise from them will reinforce your resolve to overcome problem gambling.

Finally, use this self-help book as a resource whenever the urge to gamble rears its head, no matter how trivial it appears. Do not dismiss danger signals, for they herald a return to pain.

Useful resources

Useful reading

There are an increasing number of really good books on the treatment of problem gambling outside the field of special-ist scientific journals and conference proceedings. Useful material may be obtained from Gamblers Anonymous (see 'Useful contact sources' below) or any of the specialist gambling treatment resource centres that are now emerging in response to the recognition of the widespread welfare and social problems associated with the increased access to gambling in our communities.

For general reading on the subject, the following books are recommended:

Gainsbury, S. & Blaszczynski, A. (eds.) (2014). *Exploring Internet Gambling*. London: Routledge.

Grant, J. E. & Potenza, M. N. (eds.) (2004). *Pathological Gambling: A clinical guide to treatment*. Washington, DC: American Psychiatric Publishing.

Kennerley, H. (1997). *Overcoming Anxiety: A self-help guide using cognitive behavioural techniques*. London: Robinson,

2014. (For a complete list of books in this series, and especially for the titles *Overcoming Panic*, *Overcoming Depression* and *Overcoming Low Self-esteem*, see the series list at the front of this book.)

Ladouceur, R., Sylvain, C., Boutin, C. & Doucet, C. (2002). *Understanding and Treating the Pathological Gambler*. New York: Wiley & Sons.

Lesieur, H. (1984). *The Chase*. Cambridge, Mass.: Schenkman.

Miller, W. R. & Rollnick, S. (2013). *Motivational Interviewing: Helping people change* (3rd ed.). New York: Guilford Press.

Petry, N. M. (2005). *Pathological Gambling: Etiology, comorbidity, and treatment*. Washington, DC: American Psychological Association.

Richard, D., Blaszczynski, A. & Nower, L. (eds.) (2014). *The Wiley-Blackwell Handbook of Disordered Gambling*. Oxford: Wiley-Blackwell.

Smith, G., Hodgins, D. C. & Williams, R. J. (eds.) (2007). *Research and Measurement Issues in Gambling Studies*. New York: Academic Press.

Walker, M. (1992). *The Psychology of Gambling*. Oxford: Pergamon Press.

Zangeneh, M., Blaszczynski, A. & Turner, N. (eds.) (2008). *In the Pursuit of Winning: Problem gambling theory, research and treatment*. New York: Springer.

Zangeneh, M., Blaszczynski, A. & Turner, N. (2005). (eds.). *Problem Gambling: A multidisciplinary textbook*. Toronto: PAS e-Publishing Services.

Other books describing personal accounts and the impact of gambling disorders are also available at local or online bookstores.

The following more specialist works, describing early accounts of gambling, are also cited in the text:

Day, John I. (1950). 'Horse Racing and the Pari-mutuel', *Annals of the American Academy of Political and Social Science*, pp. 55–61.

France, Clemens J. (1902). 'The Gambling Impulse', *American Journal of Psychology*, pp. 364–76.

Langer, E. J. (1975). 'The Illusion of Control', *Journal of Personality and Social Psychology*, pp. 311–28.

Peterson, Virgil W. (1950). 'Obstacles to Enforcement of Gambling Laws', *Annals of the American Academy of Political and Social Science*, pp. 9–20.

Squires, P. (1937). 'Fyodor Dostoevsky: A Psychopathographical Sketch', *Psychoanalytic Review*, pp. 365–88.

There are also a number of specialist scientific journals devoted to the study of gambling and addictive behaviours:

Addiction
International Gambling Studies
Journal of Gambling Studies
Psychology of Addictive Behaviors

Useful contact sources

The best way to find a service in your locality is via an online search using the term, 'problem gambling treatment services'. Relevant telephone helpline services in your location may also direct you to specialist services.

Great Britain

Gamblers Anonymous
Look on the website for information on your nearest meeting.

GamCare
2nd Floor, 7–11 St John's Hill
London SW11 1TR

Canada

Provinces in Canada offer counselling services. Search websites for available services in each province. Two websites provide useful information:

Gambling Research Exchange Ontario:
www.greo.ca/

Problem Gambling Institute of Ontario:
www.problemgambling.ca

United States of America

National Council on Problem Gambling
PO Box 9419
Washington DC 20016
ncgc@ncpgambling.org

Australia

Gamblers Anonymous

Each state and territory has specialist gambling counsellors funded by their respective government. These can be found on their respective government websites.

Gambler's Help is a national telephone helpline for gamblers on 1800 858 858. The helpline will direct callers to their closest counselling service.

Asia

Singapore: National Council on Problem Gambling: www.ncpg.org.sg

A number of counselling services for gambling are also available in Hong Kong and Macau.

Europe

It is best to search the websites for gambling counselling services available in each country.

Extra monitoring sheets

Daily monitoring sheet

Date: .... Day: ....

1	2	3	4	5	6	7	8
Time and place	Feelings and thoughts before gambling (rating of tension on ten-point scale – 1 = low, 10 = high)	Borrowings	Cash at start of session	Cash at end of session	Win	Loss	Feelings associated with results (rating of tension on ten-point scale – 1 = low, 10 = high)
Total wins/losses and borrowings							

Daily monitoring sheet

Date: .... Day: ....

1	2	3	4	5	6	7	8
Time and place	Feelings and thoughts before gambling (rating of tension on ten-point scale – 1 = low, 10 = high)	Borrowings	Cash at start of session	Cash at end of session	Win	Loss	Feelings associated with results (rating of tension on ten-point scale – 1 = low, 10 = high)
Total wins/losses and borrowings							

Daily monitoring sheet

Date: .... Day: ....

1	2	3	4	5	6	7	8
Time and place	Feelings and thoughts before gambling (rating of tension on ten-point scale – 1 = low, 10 = high)	Borrowings	Cash at start of session	Cash at end of session	Win	Loss	Feelings associated with results (rating of tension on ten-point scale – 1 = low, 10 = high)
Total wins/losses and borrowings							

Daily monitoring sheet

Date: .... Day: ....

1	2	3	4	5	6	7	8
Time and place	Feelings and thoughts before gambling (rating of tension on ten-point scale – 1 = low, 10 = high)	Borrowings	Cash at start of session	Cash at end of session	Win	Loss	Feelings associated with results (rating of tension on ten-point scale – 1 = low, 10 = high)
Total wins/losses and borrowings							

Daily monitoring sheet

Date: .... Day: ....

1	2	3	4	5	6	7	8
Time and place	Feelings and thoughts before gambling (rating of tension on ten-point scale – 1 = low, 10 = high)	Borrowings	Cash at start of session	Cash at end of session	Win	Loss	Feelings associated with results (rating of tension on ten-point scale – 1 = low, 10 = high)
Total wins/losses and borrowings							

Daily monitoring sheet

Date: .... Day: ....

1	2	3	4	5	6	7	8
Time and place	Feelings and thoughts before gambling (rating of tension on ten-point scale – 1 = low, 10 = high)	Borrowings	Cash at start of session	Cash at end of session	Win	Loss	Feelings associated with results (rating of tension on ten-point scale – 1 = low, 10 = high)
Total wins/losses and borrowings							

Running summary of weekly activities

Date: .... Week: ....

Date	Wins	Losses
Day 1		
Day 2		
Day 3		
Day 4		
Day 5		
Day 6		
Day 7		
Total		

Index